This book is dedicated to the man who helped me find 'US' ~ Unique Solutions ~ my husband of 36 years, Peter Crumpacker. Thank you for loving me and being open to working through every single breakdown to get to a breakthrough. You have given me more freedom than I could ever have alone because you have supported my vision for all these years! I will love you forever!

The Journey to US is a book for couples, or for people who want to improve any relationship they are in, a friendship, a familial or even a work relationship. This book will also be helpful for those who want to create a new romantic relationship or figure out why the last ones did not work out.

Feel free to contact me to let me know how the book supported you. I am also available as a life coach.

www.thejourneytoUS.com

Chapter 1

INTENTION

You are the creator of your relationship. You are creating exactly what you intend to create. If you believe that there is something more, different or better that you want, then YOU must BE something more, different or better. You are the creator.

There are payoffs and prices to every aspect of your relationship, even the parts you don't like. EG: If my partner is distant and unresponsive the payoff is that you get to have an excuse to make choices that you wouldn't make if you had no complaints. The prices are, ever growing distance that may lead to the demise of the relationship.

Sometimes we settle as we think it is easier than being honest with ourselves as to what we really want.

Maybe we settle because we don't know how to change things.

Maybe we settle because we are unwilling to act to create the relationship of our dreams because we want to avoid conflict. Maybe we settle because we are unwilling to get uncomfortable. We don't want to argue but resentment builds if we are not growing closer.

Avoiding dealing with our needs or desires usually just delays the inevitable argument. We are afraid of discontent instead of embracing it and using it to see there is something else we can create - WITH LOVE. We believe we need to be angry to demand change, that belief destroys relationships. Plus, it is not even true.

Most of your beliefs about relationships and your partner are not true; we are making them all up. Even the beliefs that you have a lot of evidence about may just be what you have made up in order to stay comfortable.

So, your first task is to get very clear on your intention. What do you want? Decide right now what your intentions are for this relationship, no matter what the circumstances, challenges or breakdowns may come, what do you want?

Keep asking yourself that question and get a Journal, you will need one to get through this book, and write, down what you want for your relationship. Be brave, be bold and be honest, what do you really want? Even if you think it is not possible, write down what you want to create with your partner. Write what the very best possible relationship would look like. Don't think about the difficulties or the circumstances in the way, just think about what you want and write it down.

Story # 1. Importance of Intention

It is important that you have a vision for your relationship and your partner does also and that you share it with each other.

Years ago, I had a couple in the Loving Couples course which is where I taught the tools that are in this book and learned so much from other couples.

One couple had a big age gap which doesn't always matter but in this case it did. Her vision was a family, a house, a picket fence and stability. His vision was to get a motorcycle and ride, live on the road, camp out see the world as far as you could go in every direction with no ties. When they shared their vision with each other and the class it was obvious that one of them would have to give up their vision to be with each other.

Neither of them was willing to give up their vision. They went their separate ways but both of them were glad that they had not wasted years figuring out that they had a totally different vision.

GET COMMITTED TO YOUR INTENTION!

Caution: write ONLY what you want, NOT what you don't want, for example:

~~I don't want my partner to cheat on me~~

Should be: I want my partner to be faithful

~~I don't want to get a divorce~~

I want us to stay together for life.

Think of it like this; you need to only write what you want as the universe does not recognize "don't" or "not" so whatever you write you are manifesting according to the law of attraction; from the books "The Secret" and "The Four Agreements."

If the universe does not recognize "don't" those two statements crossed out above would actually manifest a cheating partner and a divorce. This exercise is about what you DO want.

Some people live in a state of fear instead of love. They are always afraid of what they don't want and therefore it is what they focus on and what they look for and what they manifest. It will be new to flip that coin every time you think about what you are afraid of and instead focus on what you DO want.

Fear: I don't want you to go out.

Truth: I want to spend more time with you

Fear: I don't want you to spend more money.

Truth: I want us to both be on the same page about our finances so that we can make responsible decisions.

Before you speak, before making any requests or before criticizing get clear on what your fear is, then ask yourself, "If I were choosing to come from LOVE instead of fear, what would I be saying differently."

JOURNAL:

What do you want for your relationship before moving forward. Write down everything you can think of that you want in your relationship.

Ask yourself this: Would working on that vision create closeness or distance?

OK, once you know what you want and you have written it down, then we can get about the process of creating it.

Now be really brave and ask your partner to write down a list of what they want too. Share what you both wrote with each other. Make sure to be open when you read the list. It may be a surprise. Do your best not to judge or take anything personally.

We have a tremendous amount of really effective tools for you. Even if these exercises in this book stir things up, trust the process. In order to create anything that you want, you must be willing to get uncomfortable and do some things differently.

NOW CREATE AN INTENTION STATEMENT

Write down what both of you agree that you want for this relationship. Combine both lists leaving out, for now, anything that you are not both in total agreement with, for example: Let's say one of you likes to go on wild exciting adventures together and the other person is a homebody who likes to spend weekends home alone together watching movies and cuddling. Both of those things may work occasionally, but neither would work all the time.

I count my blessings because my husband and I are very different. As I write this book, my sweet husband and I have been together for thirty-six years. After four months of a long-distance romance, we moved in together having only spent eleven physical days together. We have been through a lot, and each stage of our marriage has brought us closer and wiser. I am the kite, and he is the anchor. I listen to my gut, and he listens to his brain. I am the traveler, and he is the homebody. I like being alone, and he likes being around people. I am spiritual, and he is a nature boy. I burn hard boiled eggs until they turn into little baby bombs, he is a gourmet cook. I can handle a ton of stress, and any drama makes him sweat. He loves boating, and when I am out in a boat, I feel like a refugee just praying to get to land. I love shopping in cute, quaint stores in little old towns. He feels like a little kid who just dropped to the floor, still holding his Mom's hand, and now needs to be dragged. I like to purge, and he likes to 'collect.' I am direct, and he is tactful. But over the years since we decided to support each other's "adventures," I am way more willing to go out and actually enjoy the boat and he is now enjoying exploring old towns and talking to people, that is what he likes to do. There are only two things we completely agree on, our children and our politics. That has been more than enough to keep us loving each other for thirty-six years. Has it been easy? NO! But easy bores me. It's been an adventure! Thanks for loving me, Pete.

So, the one thing in my life that has been very important to me is freedom. Marriage and I didn't seem to work out well because as soon as I felt controlled or unable pursue my own vision for my life, I no longer wanted to be married to the person who was in my way.

When I met my present husband, I was twenty-nine years old. I had a seven-year-old daughter, and I had just done some powerful transformational personal growth work that ignited my vision. Instead of taking away my freedom, this man actually afforded me more freedom by supporting my dreams.

Some of my dreams have been less than sensible. About twenty-five years ago, after working very hard in Commercial Real Estate, I decided to leave a job that paid very well to start a personal growth company because I wanted to make a difference more than I wanted to make a lot of money. Even though I only made about 20% of what I used to earn my husband supported me at 100% because he saw how happy I was and the difference my work was making. Our intention for our relationship was to support each other's vision.

So, now, combine your lists to make an "INTENTION FOR YOUR RELATIONSHIP" and hang a copy on the bathroom wall, so you get to read it and remind yourself every day what your intention is.

Chapter 2
THE PROCESS OF CREATION

We are like a big human magnet; we are constantly magnetizing experiences to ourselves. I call that being the "source." The thing that determines what we have in our life is what we put out into the world and into our lives and relationships. This is the universal law of attraction. Probably the most common reminder we have heard is: "What you shall sow, so you shall reap."

BEING THE CREATOR:
1. Use what you DON'T want to realize what you DO want. It is through contrast that we find our path.
2. Make sure you verbalize only what you DO want.
3. Know what you do want. Consciously dwell on it.
4. Envision what you want. Feel it (not think) with all of your senses hearing, taste, smell and sight.
5. Get excited about having it. Passion is what creates. Be grateful that it is coming even with no evidence.
6. Declare what you want to create every day, in a Journal or to your partner or a coach or a friend.

Make a date to watch the movie "The Secret" together. Pause the movie whenever you want to talk about what comes up for you. That will be a very valuable evening!

Story # 2: MOVE THE POLE,
A story about clear intention.

Several years ago, my husband and I went to Hawaii to visit our daughter who lived there with her husband and their little daughter. My son-in-law is in the Navy and they were stationed there. They loved Hawaii and even though they were to be transferred to Jacksonville, FL for three years, I knew they would want to return to Hawaii as soon as they could choose their next duty station.

On the way home from Hawaii my husband and I discussed how we could support them in buying a home in Hawaii. We decided to buy an investment property on the island where we lived in Florida, so we could build equity over a few years and later use that as a down payment for a house in Hawaii.

We found a tiny, old, run down duplex very near our home that we could afford. As we looked around the property we noticed that there was a huge power pole in the back yard only a foot away from the screened porch. It had a massive transformer at the top of the pole, which dangled directly over the porch roof and made a loud buzzing noise. I pointed out this invading giant pole to my husband and he grimaced and said, "Maybe we shouldn't buy this place." "Don't worry," I told him, "I'll get it moved." The next-door neighbor was peeking over the fence like Wilson on the old TV show, "Home Improvement."

He overheard me and chuckled as he said, "Lady, everyone who has ever owned that place has tried to get that pole moved and couldn't do it." "Ah," I said, "but they just 'tried' -- I, on the other hand, have a Clear Intention; I'm moving the pole!"

I called the electric company and asked them, "Who moves poles?" "No one," was their answer, "We don't move poles." "I understand," I continued, "but I am moving a large power pole with a huge transformer on the top of it and I need help, so who should I talk to?" At this point they thought I was some crazy lady with a chain saw, so they quickly connected me with a guy in charge of poles; we'll call him Willy.

I told Willy my problem and he responded, "We don't move poles." "I understand," I continued, "but I am moving a large power pole with a huge transformer on top of it and I need help, it's very heavy." Willy came right over.

We looked at the pole, discussed how its location was so incredibly inappropriate; I believe the prospect of advertising for tenants who may want experience "transformer cancer" came up too. Willy was very sympathetic and agreed that the pole never should have been put there -- but, he explained that because it had been there for over 20 years, the electric company had what was called "prescriptive rights" so they did not have to move it.

I acknowledged that I understood and accepted that Willy did not have the authority to move the pole, but I knew that he was aware of the person who could get it moved. He nodded and told me to call the electric company on Monday and ask for his supervisor, Jim. "Great," I said, "but let's see if he is free right now -- what's his cell number?"

"Jim," I said, after reaching him on his cell, "I am here with Willy -- great guy, by the way -- and we have a big pole with a transformer on it and we need to move it, but we need your help; it's heavy."

Jim was picturing Willy being held hostage by a crazy lady with a chain saw, he showed up fifteen minutes later. All three of us stared at the pole and finally Jim said, "OK, lady, we can move the pole, but you will need to pay for it."

"Awesome! So, we have established the fact that you CAN move it, great! But I'm not going to pay for it, so let's keep thinking!"

We all stared a little longer and suddenly, Jim pointed in the air at the wire coming from the buzzing transformer. "Lady, do you see that wire?" "Yes," I said, excited at his breakthrough tone. "That wire goes to your neighbor Wilson's house; we are not allowed to run a wire over your property to service another property! WE'RE MOVING THE POLE!" Jim exclaimed.

Jim "high fived" me, I "high fived" Willy, and Willy "high fived" Jim. Out of my clear intention, the electric company moved the pole; and out of my clear intention we gained enough equity in three years for my daughter and son-in-law to be able buy a townhouse on Oahu, big enough for the in-laws to visit, too.

The moral of the story is that with Clear Intention ANYTHING is possible! Now, go take action on your dreams!

IT MATTERS AS MUCH AS YOU SAY IT DOES

Chapter 3.

PURPOSE OF RELATIONSHIP

Hollywood has us believing that all relationships are supposed to be 'happily ever after,' they are supposed to be easy and ever reflective of the Love you first found in each other eyes. The TV writers want us to think that if we do ever have a conflict, it's supposed to be funny and trivial like in the sit-coms. BOLOGNA!! The purpose of being in a committed relationship is to create challenges for ourselves and each other, to be a protagonist toward our own personal growth.

With a partner, we have more opportunity to grow in love, wisdom, and vulnerability. That's why we sometimes see couples who never argue break up after years, because there is no challenge! Somewhere along the line they stopped being each other's protagonist.

A protagonist will stand for you to be your highest and best self, a protagonist will call you out if you are not taking care of yourself, a protagonist will support you in going for your dreams. Before you can expect your partner to be a better protagonist for you, you must be a better protagonist for them.

THANK YOU FOR BEING MY PROTAGONIST

There is a big difference between being a nag than in being a protagonist. A nag is bugging you to do what you don't want to do, what they want you to do. A protagonist talks to you about your vision for your career, your health, your relationships, the difference you want to make and the experiences you want in your life. A protagonist will stand for you to create your vision.

Whatever piece of that vision you are aware of, that your partner has, start there and BE their protagonist by asking them how you can support them.

When you feel your partner is supporting your dreams it is important to acknowledge that, just say "Thank you for being my protagonist" so they know you appreciate them encouraging you and taking a stand for you. Someday they may say the same thing to you.

Remember: You always need to be the first one to make the changes you want. Your partner is just responding to you. This is my version of the serenity prayer:

"God, grant me the serenity to accept the people I cannot change, the courage to change the one I can, and the wisdom to know it's ME."

If you don't like how your partner is reacting to you then YOU need to act differently. Everyone in your life, partner, children, co-workers, they are all just in reaction to YOU. You ACT differently, they will react differently. It's like magic. You are in complete control.

*Protagonist: a person who causes or forwards action

JOURNAL:

How can I be a loving protagonist for my partner?

How would I like my partner to be a protagonist for me?

To be an effective protagonist you may need to break the cycle of co-dependency. Co-dependency is usually described as "If they FEEL bad, then I feel bad, and I have to fix it so they FEEL better." Co-dependency can also look like "If I FEEL bad, I want them to know about it and FEEL bad too, and I'll make sure they do!"
In the suggested reading at the end of this book I mention an author that addresses co-dependency in a very effective manner.

CHAPTER 4.

EGO OVER ESSENCE

One of the tactics we use to protect our vulnerable pure essence is to wear masks; images that disguise who we really are. The EGO is the keeper of these masks and of our underlying conversations, fears or limiting beliefs about ourselves. EG: I'm unworthy, unlovable, incapable.

The problem occurs when the image, the façade we hide behind, takes over the essence such that the authentic self is put into hibernation. Many of us wear a mask and our mask falls in love with someone else's mask. Then we are surprised when the mask falls off and the real genuine person emerges.

We have a belief that we are supposed to look a certain way, have certain accomplishments or have acquired certain 'stuff.' Our ego tells us we are in competition with others and our value depends on winning whatever the game is that we made up.

One of the ways we enter into relationships that are destined to be difficult is when we are interacting while under the influence of alcohol/drugs. That mask hides who we truly are, under that mask our essence no longer exists, only the drug exists.

The way to wake up the genuine, authentic self is to rip off the masks that prevent the light from shining. Marianne Williamson wrote a wonderful essay in one of her many poignant books that address "the light." She starts out saying: "It is not our darkness that we fear; it is our light." When we remember who we are and how immeasurably powerful we are, then we can no longer waste that power. Even if you had a crystal ball and could see all the wondrous things that would occur in your life when you rid yourself of the masks, it may still be frightening. This next exercise is for the purpose of removing the masks that keep us from shining our light.

JOURNAL:

Write down the names of five people who you know well. They can be family, friends or co-workers. They can be living still or not.

After their names write three negative characteristics they have that mask their genuine essence; the things they use to hide their light. EG: controlling, defensive, manipulative, doormat, righteous, confused, weak, unhealthy, addicted, etc. Please complete that list before moving on.

All the characteristics that you assigned to those five people are also the masks that YOU use to hide your light. If you did not own those masks yourself, on some level, you would not be able to recognize them in others. What you dislike in others you dislike in yourself even more. Now read over the characteristics you assigned the five people you know and instead of denying that you own those traits yourself, look at where that may be true on some level.

I strongly dislike lies. I hold everyone in their highest possibility, as if they are all honest with me. When I find someone is using the mask of dishonesty I have a strong dislike for that choice. I pride myself on my honesty, even if people get angry, I am still honest. I had to look at where I was dishonest because of my strong dislike for the mask of lies; I must own it on some level. It was not an easy introspection, but I finally realized that I sometimes get so passionate in my story telling that I tend to embellish with my own filters and interpretations in order to make a point. That can be seen, by the people who witnessed the same event as I did, as dishonest, as they have very different filters and interpretations as I do. To be completely honest I would declare what was fact and what was interpretation. I also have found myself withholding information if I was avoiding hurting someone or avoiding creating an unnecessary conflict, and that too is a type of dishonesty.

Some masks may apply more than others. Here is how you can tell. If you repeated the same "characteristic" more than once when doing the exercise then, look at how it applies to your masks.

Often people will be accused of being controlling or manipulative and we can brush it off, saying to ourselves "Oh, that is their stuff." Well, maybe so. If only one person brings it to your attention that you are acting like a Jack ass, stubborn and controlling, then maybe it is "their stuff." If twenty people bring it to your attention, even if it is over a long period of time, buy yourself a saddle, you are acting like a Jack ass! Remember "Jack ass" is not who you are, it is a mask you use to cover up who you truly are. We are looking at the masks for the purpose of ripping them off to reveal our true selves. Go back to your list in your Journal and circle what appears more than once to see what characteristics that may be important for you to look at in yourself.

If one of the characteristics you wrote has you be defensive, really look at that! If I told you the mask you wore is "blue bus" you may cock your head like a confused puppy but it would not make you defensive because it does not apply to you. If I said, you wear the mask of selfishness, or victim or abuser, one of them may feel insulting or put you in a state of defensiveness or protection. That is the one to look at.

Now go back to your Journal again and underline what hurts or has you feeling defensive or has you thinking "That's not right!" They are the characteristics that would be the most valuable for you to look at if you want to grow into the person you want to be. If you are working on laying down that ego it will be much easier for your partner to be in a relationship with you.

When we can recognize the times that our EGO overtakes our ESSENCE then we are on the path of mastery, the path to living in a state of authenticity and vulnerability.

Dr. Wayne Dyer was a great inspiration to many people, including me. He said that EGO stands for Edging God Out. I was meditating on this concept one day, and somehow the mathematician in me came out to play.

If EGO = Edging God Out
And GOD = LOVE
Then EGO = Edging (Love) Out
Therefore EGO = FEAR.
I choose love, (Essence) not fear.

Remember, assessing whether you are in a state of Ego or Essence is YOUR job, no one else's. Also, it is not your job to judge or assess where anyone else is in their Journey of Ego or Essence, especially your partner. These tools are for YOU to use to be the best version of yourself, not to use to attempt to change your partner.

WHAT'S THE DIFFERENCE?

EGO:
Edging God Out ~
Disconnected, denying, defending, justifying, analyzing, fear of mistakes or being wrong, being a victim, angry, blaming, powerless, protected, fake, guarded, awkward, isolated, bigoted, judgmental, closed, resentful, unaware.

ESSENCE:
Energizing ~ focusing on, accepting, noticing
Spiritual ~ higher power connection, soul connection
Senses ~ intuition, mindfulness, divine wisdom
Empowering ~ causes, effects, creates, opens
Natural ~ authentic, genuine, childlike, knowing
Connective ~ oneness, accepting, present
Enlightenment ~ awareness, discovery, choice

Recognition: The first step to transcending the Ego, so that you release your pure essence to take over as the leader of your life, is to recognize the difference between them. This process reminds me of Nelson Mandela's Journey. The collective Ego of South Africa imprisoned the true leader of South Africa, but he still existed. When his stand and his intention were unwavering, even behind bars, the essence was finally released to lead!

EGO:	ESSENCE:
human flesh	spiritual being
instinct	intuition
survival	guidance
pain/pleasure	experience
unconscious	conscious
victim	creator
feelings driven	commitment driven
fear based	love based

Ego is about Human Flesh, all things that are sensuous; sight, smell, taste, touch, sound. What is pleasurable for just the receiver.

Essence is about the spiritual being, all things that exist, even beyond death: character, connection, oneness, divinity, peacefulness.

Ego is driven by instinct; what the cave men used to defend themselves and conquer perceived threats upon them. This is what makes us warriors.

Essence is about intuition, natural knowing and a calm centeredness that allows us to trust ourselves.

Ego is about survival, scrounging and foraging in a state of scarcity, believing that there is not enough to go around, panicking while hoarding and protecting what is mine.

Essence is about guidance, trusting that we are always being guided by our divine wisdom and our vision. Following that guidance attracts abundance, promotes sharing and supports a win-win atmosphere that leads to oneness.

Ego is about avoiding pain and seeking pleasure. This encourages withholding or lying to avoid pain. Seeking pleasure can lead to promiscuity that would put our relationship in jeopardy.

Essence is about experiencing life fully, living in the moment, seeing all the gifts that surround us. When we are willing to experience all of life we become a more well-rounded, empathetic, understanding, adventurer.

**WHAT IS YOUR INTENTION?
CLOSENESS OR DISTANCE?**

Ego also has us be unconscious that we are unconscious. We may at times become conscious that we are unconscious but we will protect ourselves from exploring what's beyond that in a state of Ego, unwilling to grow, see, or know anything other than what we already know.

Essence is a state of consciousness; first becoming conscious that there is somewhere else to ascend to in life that would be fulfilling, then achieving that ascension, followed by living in that state, then eventually existing there as routine or normal, unconsciously.

Ego: Unconscious that I am unconscious (Duh.)
Ego: Conscious that I am unconscious (Huh?)
Essence: Conscious that I am conscious (Oh!)
Essence: Unconscious that I am conscious (Ohm)

Ego is the perpetual victim, always taking everything personally, blaming, defending and making excuses, being the superior, right, taken advantage of, Teflon person.

Essence is the creator, all-powerful, in control of themselves, seeing the possibility, using all results as feedback from which to learn and grow. Essence is always willing to make new choices that lead them closer to their vision and the greater good.

Ego is feelings driven, succumbing to all carnal desire, whim, and emotion that feeds selfish desires.

Essence is commitment driven, willing to sacrifice the unimportant immediate gratification to support the big picture, the vision, the intention.

Ego is fear based, consumed with winning at all costs, making everyone else lose, hoarding resources, hiding knowledge or information, protecting by lashing out at anyone who is different, looking for people or things to judge, criticize or despise.

Essence is love based, devoted to being in service wherever possible, being willing to be used for the greater good. Essence lives as an unceasing contribution.

WHEN AM I THERE?

Discernment: The Ego can identify, judge and point out when other people are in a state of Ego. The Essence recognizes itself; the essence feels at home in any situation, with any other people. The essence does not judge, the essence accepts and finds all human beings very interesting. The essence sees the light in people and that's all. The essence holds everyone in their highest possibility including themselves.

One way of discerning where you are may be to check in with your feelings as they are a valuable indicator as to who is in charge, your Ego or your Essence.

Embracing your Essence as a way of life is a Journey of choices and awareness. No one can be here at all times unless you live in a state of constant meditation. St. Francis said "Pray unceasingly," and that is what living in a state of pure essence is. I am not there, and I seriously doubt that I ever will be, but the Essence does not judge the Journey, and I AM there. I have times when I succumb to the selfishness of Ego and make my feelings too important. It is not bad or wrong, it just "is." Noticing it gives me a vehicle to escape the Ego and to choose Essence instead at some point.

JOURNAL:

When the Ego is the captain of the ship we may experience these feelings below. Write about any times or situations when you remember experiencing the feelings below. Take your time, really think about each group, this will show you what people places and things trigger your ego:

- Disconnection, loneliness, superiority.
- Heavy, dense, anchored, held down by lead weights.
- Expectation, "If it's to be it's up to someone else"
- Blame, resentment, entitlement, closed.
- Need to Control, force, threaten, manipulate, intimidate.
- Fear of obliteration, death, failure, loss, intimidation.
- Stress, drama, chaos, confusion.
- Need to know "how," unsure, insecure, paralyzed.
- Fear of being victimized, used or taken advantage of.
- Needing the tangible, superficial, shallow.
- Craving what satisfies the flesh, selfishly.
- Unsatisfied when arriving at the destination.
- Still searching for contentment in the end.

JOURNAL:
When you put the Essence is in control of the ship we may experience these feelings below. Write about any times or situations when you remember experiencing these feelings, take your time, really think about each group, this will show you what people places and things support your essence:

- Deep connection including cellular memories, past lives.
- God force within, a universal spiritual oneness with all.
- Intention as a life force, being the source, the cause.
- Trust of the process, being guided by Divine wisdom.
- Using each experience to learn and grow.
- Taking global responsibility.
- Acceptance of what is in the now.
- Embracing change, shifting.
- Accepting new challenges as exciting.
- Peaceful, calm, at true home no matter where you are.
- Being guided, a part of the Divine order, having intuition.
- Having grace, lightness, serenity, natural knowing.
- Identifying with Saints, Mystics, Oracles, healers.
- Willingness to be used as a vessel, a conduit through which a higher power is invited.
- Being in the moment, delighted with small things.
- Adventurer on the Journey, growing, in the process.
- If we were in a state of essence with our partner, would that create closeness or distance?

WHAT DOES THIS HAVE TO DO WITH MY RELATIONSHIP? Everything.

No one who is living an authentic life wants to be in a relationship with someone's Ego, it affects every area of your life when you are not living as your essence, your genuine self. Here is how it affects even your sex life:

SEXUAL PARADIGM FOR THE EVOLVED COUPLE
EGO DRIVEN SEXUAL PARADIGM

One partner feels neglected
One partner feels pressured

One partner feels unsatisfied with frequency
One partner feels unappreciated

One partner wants the other to just know they want sex
One partner needs time to mentally prepare for sex

One partner is irritated that they don't get enough
One partner feels abused by the demand

One partner expects the other to be the aggressor
One partner feels burdened with the expectation

One partner focuses on their needs and desires
One partner feels used and disconnected

One partner feels undesirable without sex
One partner uses excuses to avoid sex

One partner attempts to blame the other
One partner feels guilty and manipulated

One partner uses sex as a tool to control
One partner uses sex as a weapon to punish

One partner equates sex with self-worth,
attractiveness
One partner equates sex with duty, obligation

One partner wants a mate to initiate sex, fear of
rejection
One partner is burdened by always needing to
initiate sex

ESSENCE DRIVEN SEXUAL PARADIGM

Each partner takes responsibility to create
encounters
Each partner communicates what they need and
want

Each partner makes dates for intimacy or romance
Each partner makes dates for sexual encounters

Each partner expresses their desire for closeness
Each partner shows appreciation for their mate

Each partner expresses concerns and feelings
Each partner accepts the other's feelings

Each partner feels free to ask for time and space
Each partner wants to give what their mate needs

Each partner can offer affection with no agenda
Each partner can be spontaneous when nurtured

Each partner can be gentle, patient and create
safety
Each partner can be free, passionate and vulnerable

Each partner is willing to work on repairing old
wounds
Each partner is willing to release past breakdowns

Each partner can express historical fears about
intimacy
Each partner is aware that their past does not own
them

Each partner can depend on their mate for
acceptance
Each partner can trust and be trusted and
understood

Each partner can create fun, romantic, adventurous
dates
Each partner can speak from the heart and truly
listen

Each partner can learn together and share their
learning
Each partner owns his or her experience as the
creator

Each partner is responsible for creating what they want

Each partner knows their mate may have different needs

HOW DO I JOURNEY TO THE OTHER SIDE?

The Ego is usually in the question "HOW do I shift" or "what do I need to DO"?

Often, we use these unanswered questions to avoid creating results. "I don't know HOW" or "I'm not sure what to DO" so we take no action at all.

Transitioning from Ego to Essence takes choosing a way of being and a belief system or a 'paradigm' that supports your authentic self. Now having said that here are some things you can "DO" to learn "HOW" to make the shift:

AWARENESS: Become aware of which state you are in, Ego or Essence. Just accept where you are at any given moment without judgment. Know what triggers your ego and nurtures your essence and share that with your partner.

GRATITUDE PRAYERS: Spend any idle time focusing on all the people, experiences and things that you are grateful for, the more appreciation you experience the more you will attract to be thankful for. Tell your partner every day something that you are grateful for about them.

BREATHING EXERCISES: Spend a few minutes whenever possible to concentrate on your breathing, take three deep breaths and slowly release them as you visualize your breath cleansing first your body, then your mind and finally your spirit.

DETOXIFY YOUR BODY: Eliminate toxic foods, processed foods, meats, sugar, alcohol, drink water that is purified, add antioxidant foods to your diet, take vitamins, use natural and herbal medicine when possible. This is a process, just make one improvement at a time. You are a work in progress, a masterpiece.

YOGA / TAI CHI / QIGONG: Learn one new pose per week and spend time practicing the poses every day. Even ten minutes a day of Yoga, Tai Chi or Qigong will bring you closer to your Essence. The ancient people who found personal power through these disciplines have passed their wisdom on to us. Alternate the practice of each one as a way to expand your opportunities to connect with your Essence. Just even one simple pose a day will work.

ONE WITH NATURE: Commune with a tree, spend time focusing on your favorite tree, it may have a message for you. One of the insights of mastery is to become one with nature.

WALKING: The benefits of walking are countless. Walking supports your body mind and spirit and gives you the opportunity to breathe, commune with nature, detoxify your body through blood circulation, time for reflecting on your awareness and your ability to walk is one more thing to add to your gratitude list. Walking with your partner creates a healthy connection.

REIKI: Learn about, study and experiment with your ability to send healing energy to others. When you are connected to your partner, you can feel each other's healing energy when sick or injured.

MEDITATING: Explore different forms of meditation. All the great Masters who transcended their Ego used the practice of meditation, hence the name "Transcendental Meditation." Meditating together with your partner is fabulous but meditating alone is powerful too.

_____

JOURNAL:

What will you do this week to nurture your ability to be in a state of essence?

Do you think these methods of working on being your true essence will create closeness or distance with your partner?

_____

SURRENDERING TO THE ESSENCE:

The best meditation for you is led by you. For this next exercise you will need a way to record your own voice and play back the recording. You can read this over some soft instrumental music and listen to it as a guide to your own personal meditation. Pause between each sentence. Add anything that you believe would be helpful to unfold your pure essence.

JUST "BEING" MEDITATION

I close my eyes as I sit in a comfortable position. I can move, yawn or stir at any time but I keep my eyes closed so that I can maintain my level of meditation. I notice my breathing. I feel air fill my lungs. It infuses lightness into my body. I notice my body and I surround it with the white light of pure unconditional love. Whatever is not compatible with my pure essence melts away under the warmth of this light. I feel the energy of my pure essence. It feels radiant and weightless. As I concentrate on my spiritual being I feel myself expanding. My pure essence now touches the earth and becomes a beam of light that permeates the ground and infiltrates every layer of the earth. My energy reaches the center of the earth and the molten core infuses my essence with the power of connection to all earthly beings. As my energy expands it reaches out to every surface of the planet.

I now connect with every sea creature as my essence breaks through the ocean beds. I am now a part of every whale, fish, octopus, starfish, and crustacean. I am one with the sea. My spirit is the energy of pure love and light touches and infuses peace into every creature. The ocean water carries this pure light of love to every corner of the seas around the globe. My essence now moves toward the atmosphere of the earth. As my energy breaks through the soil, I connect with every blade of grass, every tree, every plant, and every flower. My pure spirit envelops every species of vegetation with energy and healing. I am now one with prairies, deserts, rain forests, mountain ranges, and farmland. Peace comes through me to every growing thing from clover in the fields to giant redwoods. My spirit now is drawn towards all other sentient souls. My essence becomes enmeshed with every insect and animal on the planet. I exist now on the planes of Africa in the Jungles and the forests. I am part of every beast free and caged. I feel the experience of oneness with all the creatures of the world. They feel the presence of love and peace through their connection with my energy. The higher consciousness of my essence now seeks out other spirits on a human Journey. My light becomes bonded with the light of every spiritual being living now. We become one. We are connected from Asia to Australia to Samoa to Europe. We are each bolstered by the love and peace that connects us.

Our respective spirits are strengthened and energized by a sense of wholeness that can only exist through the connection. I experience the paradox of unique identity and simultaneous oneness. Our union frees us all as pure love and peaceful acceptance. The combining of these magnified pure essences creates access to a higher power, an almighty being that can be reached through the merger of all spirit. I am now connected with all heavenly energy that has ever existed. I am one with God. I am one with love. I am one with everything pure. I see my own face reflected in the face of God. My soul is flawless. My aura is the color of unconditional love; I am. As I open my eyes I remain pure essence.

Affirmation for living as your Essence:
As my authentic self I am connected with all living things, all sentient souls and with my higher power. This connection is the source of love.

We just need to BE our Essence, model it and shift from ego to essence every time we become aware that we have missed the mark. The word "sin" is from Latin, and the literal translation is "missing the mark." Whenever we exit the essence to allow the ego to reign we "miss the mark."

PERPETUAL BEING

St. Francis of Assisi advised his followers to "pray unceasingly." I believe that is akin to perpetually being your pure essence. Maybe the only one who will achieve that is some shaman in a cave somewhere sitting cross legged and drawing all nutrition from the air he breaths. Accomplishing it and striving for it is like the difference between perfection and excellence. Existing and relating to others as my pure Essence is parallel to living in a state of perpetual prayer. Here I can explore my Spiritual Journey.

I have known people who constantly strove for perfection. That goal ensured disconnected relationships with the very people the perfectionist was attempting to impress. The need to be perfect is like an incubator for stress and therefore creates illness. The need for perfection is Ego based and comes with a daily session of self-punishment as the desired result is never achieved. The Ego thrives on this failure as when we are in pain the Ego is more alive.

Excellence, on the other hand, comes with enough humility to know that even our best will never be perfect. As pure essence, we know and love that about ourselves and our partners. Being mindful in our endeavor to recognize who is steering the ship, Ego or Essence, opens up choices for us. The more we choose Essence, the easier and more automatic it becomes just to BE our authentic selves.

Affirmation for igniting intuition:
I am a spiritual being who is guided by intuition. I
am conscious of my choices. I use my results and
experiences as feedback for the purpose of learning.

Moving from Ego to Essence reminds me of how a relationship develops. First, you meet and like each other, and then you have planned dates to meet. After enjoying some time together, you may decide to spend the night together. First, you bring just your toothbrush, next time some pajamas. Then a few changes of clothes come over for longer stays together. Before you know it, you are all moved in, and the cat, litter box and kitty toys come with you. But there always seems to be a few boxes at Mom's or the storage unit or your friend's garage. That is how we move from Ego to Essence, a little at a time until we are "almost" all there.

AFFIRMATION for self-acknowledgement:
I was born as pure Essence. I strive to return to my
original nature, to remember who I truly am.

Chapter 5.

EXPECTATION OR GRATITUDE

Whatever you focus on becomes all you see. Whatever story you make up becomes your truth. Whatever you believe will happen is what you will manifest.

Your entire relationship consists of a conversation, and only you are the author. Did you ever see a couple break up where one person was perfectly happy, and content and the other person said they had been miserable for years? One person focused on all the positive, loving aspects of the relationship. How wonderful it was to have a companion and someone who gave them affection and sex and made them food, brought home a paycheck and loved their children. The other person focused on what they didn't have, someone to help them more, more money, more freedom, better sex or better, interesting conversations. Of course, they were both responsible for creating what they wanted, but only one person did, the other blamed their partner for not having what they wanted.

Start by focusing on what does work, what you do love about your relationship and your partner. How different do you think your relationship and attitude would be if your focus was on what IS working instead of what you have not yet created?

JOURNAL:

Write down at least three things that are working in your relationship.
Write down at least three things that you love about your partner.
Write down at least three chores that you 'expect' your partner to handle.

EXPECTATION VS CREATING AGREEMENT

Expectation leads to disappointment. The only way you can be disappointed in another human being is if you had some expectation of them. Expectation is an unspoken desire that you believe will be fulfilled. Unspoken expectation is premeditated resentment.

The way to avoid disappointment is to make requests AND create agreement. If there is just a request or a demand with no agreement, then you will again be disappointed.

Even expecting others to keep their agreements is still expectation and it removes your responsibility in creating clear agreements and support for those agreements.

The best way to create agreements is to do the sandwich technique:

1. Acknowledge support they are giving
2. Ask for what you want specifically
3. Encourage their ability to do it

Now, ask for agreement, they may not give you agreement but at least you will have a new understanding and can either work on a win-win or work on handling your need yourself.

The two elements that damage relationships more than anything are expectation and ownership. First, we have a limiting belief that relationships are supposed to look a certain way, like my parents' or like my friends' or like movie relationships look. WE have expectations instead of communicating desires and asking for what we want so that we can design the unique relationship that works for only us, like a fingerprint. Unless you met your partner at a psychic fair, you better ask for what you want!

Then we also have 'ownership' that punctuates all these expectations. He is MY man, he should.... fill in the blank, or she is my woman, she should never.... fill in the blank.

Often, we have an "ownership" of the people in our life; MY wife, MY father, MY son, MY boss. With this "ownership" comes judgment and expectation. She was MY Mother she should have .....

We need to come to a maturity that allows everyone on our Journey to be held as a flawed human being, just fulfilling their part in our human Journey. Everyone in our life's experience has been a part of our process to learn and grow. Some people are here for very short periods of time, like the cranky waiter or the police officer who pulled us over. Some are here for a short while like our high school drama teacher or our X-relationships. Some are here for life; our partners, our children, our parents.

Often it is cultural or religious beliefs that skew our expectations too. Oh, no we are Italian, we do things like this, or no, we are this religion, so we have to do things like this. What you are doing is allowing your ancestors to decide the life, beliefs, and relationship you will have, a hundred years after they lived. Ownership is used to justify the toxicity of the expectation, and when those expectations are NOT met, we say "See, they can't be trusted." So many people say they have trust issues when in reality they have expectation issues.

When someone does not meet your expectations what that usually means is that they could not read your mind. If you have made a clear agreement and then they break their word with you then you should look and see if that person should be trusted. The truth is that everything is a negotiation, communicating what you want is imperative in the process of being the creator.

YOUR HEART WAS NEVER BROKEN
YOUR EXPECTATIONS WERE

Without expectation, we have only gratitude. My husband cooks a lot. When I come home and smell something cooking I can react in one of two ways:

#1: I expected him to cook, so I say "What's for dinner?"

#2: I have no expectations, so I say "I smell something good, what are you cooking? Thanks so much for cooking dinner! Can I help?

JOURNAL:
"Without expectation, there is only gratitude."
List all things you can think of that you are grateful for receiving from your partner.

UNSPOKEN EXPECTATIONS ARE
PREMEDITATED RESENTMENTS

Chapter 6.

RELATIONSHIP TANKS

Think of your Relationship like a gas tank. If you want to go to nice places you have to fill it with fuel. If you just ride around all day without filling the tank you will break down, run out of gas and who knows, you might be in a bad neighborhood one of those times, like divorce court!

What are some ways that we deplete our gas tanks? What are some ways that we fill those tanks up?

DEPLETE	FILL-UP
criticize	encourage
blame	be honest
break agreements	surprises
judge	touch

_____

JOURNAL:

How do you deplete your relationship tank?
How do you fill up your relationship tank?

_____

Now imagine you and your partner had been depleting the tank all week. You have been short with each other, used a surly tone of voice, been passive aggressive, been condescending, uncooperative, mean and angry. You have not touched each other or had a single kind conversation. You have yelled at each other, threatened to leave your partner, brought up their past mistakes, bullied and intimidated each other and stormed out of the house. You have told friends and relatives what a jerk your partner was, right in front of them and behind their back too. You have lied, been emotionally abusive and very distant.

Got the picture? OK. Now, after a week of that, your partner puts a dent in the new car. How do you react? Be honest, remember you both were abusing each other all week.

JOURNAL:

When breakdowns occur, and our relationship tank is empty I react like this:

My partner reacts like this:

Does that reaction create closeness or distance?

OK, it's a new week. This week you have been doing your best to create closeness instead of distance.

You have listened to your partner, been attentive and spent time with them to create emotional intimacy. You have touched them in a loving, comforting way that was just affectionate without being sexual. You have been romantic and communicated about sex and made time to have physical intimacy. You have given each other little massages all week; foot rubs, a shoulder rub, whatever you know they would appreciate. You have been accepting and non-judgmental with them, you have just agreed to disagree sometimes and let each other know that you understood their point of view even if you did not agree. You have caught them doing helpful things that you appreciate, and you have been grateful. You have really thought about the characteristics you love about each other, and you have reminded them that you "SEE" them and who they are by acknowledging those character traits you notice.

All week has been like this, just full of love and peace and support and appreciation. Now your partner smashes up the new car. How do you respond?

JOURNAL:

When breakdowns occur, and our relationship tank is full I react like this:
My partner reacts like this:
Does that reaction create closeness or distance?

INTIMACY = IN-TO-ME-SEE
Being revealing creates closeness
Withholding creates distance.
What do you want to create?
Closeness or distance?

JOURNAL:

How will I fill my partner's relationship tank?

How do I want my partner to fill my tank?

AN EXERCISE IN INTIMACY

These questions are for the purpose of creating intimacy, to reveal and to be introspective. There are no right or wrong answers.

VERY IMPORTANT: Make an agreement before doing this exercise that you will not take anything personally that your partner says that you were not expecting or do not like. This is just for the purpose of creating an understanding of each other, no agreement is necessary, just acceptance and understanding. Add questions to this list so you can do this exercise again & again, when you are out to dinner, in bed or just talking on the phone when separated. Take every opportunity to create intimacy.

Get a candle, light it, turn the lights down low and sit facing each other. Hold hands and look into each other's eyes when asking and answering the questions. If either of you feel uncomfortable, let your partner know and ask for what you need to be comfortable. For some people, intimacy is so foreign that they may only be able to handle a few questions per encounter. Make that OK, don't judge, just listen for the purpose of understanding.

INTIMACY QUESTIONS

1. I really like it when….
2. It makes me laugh when I remember….
3. I feel loved when….
4. It hurts me when….
5. One thing I'm afraid to talk about is….
6. It turns me on when you….
7. Something I'd like you to do more often is….
8. The thing that scares me the most is….
9. My discomfort about intimacy stems from….
10. You can best support me by….
11. I feel the closest too you when….
12. One thing that I have learned about you is….

Add more questions in your Journal.
Make sure you always have a candle to light.
Keep it next to your bed and light it as a sign
that you are craving some IN-2-ME-SEE!

_____

Thank your partner for participating in the
IN-TO-ME-SEE exercise and talk about
what else you could do to create intimacy.

_____

Chapter 7

CHALLENGING CONVERSATIONS

When we take each other for granted our communication sometimes becomes cavalier, condescending, brisk, cold, we seem aggravated, pre-occupied and impatient.

We tend to talk to each other while doing other things at the same time. Cooking and yelling through the pass through or getting your things together for work and muttering what you think your partner should know about that day.

Sometimes it is ok to be casual in your communication but not when there is an important, possibly volatile conversation that needs to be had.

Picture this:

You are feeling smothered and mistrusted by your partner. You know something is wrong and you are not sure what. Could you have done something that they have interpreted as a threat to the relationship? Are they feeling insecure because they are thinking about doing something that would threaten the relationship? Often people who don't trust their partner accuse them of things they are thinking of doing that themselves.

Anyway, you know something is very wrong, and you need to discuss it to change it.

Picture both of you in your bedroom, you on one side of the bed, your partner on the other side. You start talking about what is not working for you. You are both getting louder and more defensive. You are almost like boxers in the ring getting ready to fight. It feels like you should put your dukes up. You feel distant, because you are, physically and emotionally.

Now picture both of you sitting in chairs facing each other with nothing between you. You are holding hands; you are maintaining eye contact. Now you let your partner know how you have been feeling. You ask your partner how they have been feeling lately. You talk about your experience; you are revealing and ask questions that will encourage your partner to be honest and revealing. You feel connected and hopeful.

Now picture you and your partner standing close and embracing each other, like you are going to dance. Now let your partner know how you have been feeling and what you are afraid of. Hold each other as you talk, be as open and vulnerable as you can. You feel loved and safe.

Decide how you want to communicate based on the result you want to create. Yes, I know this will be uncomfortable at first. The more distant you have become the sillier this may seem. The more uncomfortable this style of communication is the more desperately your relationship needs it!

Try it. Just once, then if you need to ever do it again, it will not be as uncomfortable. You can just throw some slow music on and grab your partner to dance and just start talking. When you are heart to heart, and in each other's arms, you tend to be gentler with each other too.

Now to extend those intimacy questions we practiced in the last chapter, here are more to add to the list. These are way riskier but the more you practice honest communication the better you get at it.

1. One thing we disagree on is:
2. One thing I'm afraid will occur in this relationship is:
3. What I don't like about this relationship is:
4. What I wish we could do is:
5. What I don't like to discuss is:

Experiment:
Pick one of these questions and stand across from your partner and discuss. Stop after a few minutes and both notice how you feel.

Now sit across from each other, hold hands and discuss one of these questions. Stop after a few minutes and both notice how you feel.

Now stand, hold each other and dance while discussing one of these questions. Stop after a few minutes and both notice how you feel. Share what was different.

Journal:

How I felt when we were separate talking loudly.
How I felt when we sat together with eye contact.
How I left when we were holding each other.

**NO ONE KNOWS WHAT IT'S LIKE
TO BE THE OTHER PERSON**

Chapter 8

YOU GET BETTER AT WHATEVER YOU PRACTICE.

Here are some simple actions that you can take to improve yourself and your relationship too!

1. Work on yourself first. Whatever you know you need to work on, do it, take small steps or a giant leap, it doesn't matter. Just make some movement to be the best YOU that you can be. Get in balance. Look at the four areas of your life and get honest with yourself about what needs your attention:

    A. Look at your career, finances and education for the purpose of creating abundance or financial security. No matter your age you would benefit from having a retirement plan. If there is some other area you would rather be working in then set yourself up to be able to make that transition, when you want to, by getting the education or licensing you need to pursue the new career you want. Always have a plan "B" because you just never know what lies ahead.

    B. Look at all your relationships, not just with your partner. Make sure everyone in your life that you care about knows that you love them, so you have no regrets. Create time to spend with your loved ones that you would miss if they were gone. Develop new relationships too you never know who the next link in the chain of your life is.

C. Make sure you take care of your body, mind and spirit first of all. Like the stewardess says "Put the oxygen on yourself, first, then help everyone else!" There was one person born to take care of YOU, and that was YOU! Look at how you need to nurture your body, your mind, and your spirit to feel whole, healthy and enlightened.

D. Contribution is the one area that many people neglect because they are too busy. The problem is that ignoring this area leads to depression. If you know your life has value because you are aware that you make a difference you are energized and motivated in the other areas of your life. If you are not taking the opportunity to contribute, life can seem meaningless on those rainy days. Look for people who have less than you do and support them in seeing what is possible. "Help" is doing it for them, "Support" is empowering them to change their life themselves.

After you assess what you need to get into balance and how you will work on that, share it with your partner so they can be your protagonist and you can ask for the support you will need.

1. Make an agreed upon time to discuss important issues, timing is everything, make sure it's an agreed upon time.
    A. Ask for permission to discuss a certain subject
    B. Ask for a day and time commitment to sit down without distractions to talk
    C. Be open to renegotiating if something else comes up that needs to be handled first.

2. Make sure your intention for your relationship leads every thought, deed and action, this inspires commitment.
    A. Read your "INTENTION FOR THE RELATIONSHIP" every day and add to it when you think of something that you both want.
    B. Before having any important conversations check in with your intention for the relationship to make sure you remember with what you need to be in alignment.

3. Accept each other's feelings and opinions. Everyone has the right to feel and express whatever they need to.

A. Feelings are not right or wrong, they just are.
B. No one makes you feel anything.
C. You are in control of your feelings.
D. You have decided certain feelings are good and some are bad. Feelings are not good or bad, that is your judgement.
E. You do not have to act on your feelings.
F. Feelings are great to share to create intimacy as long as you and your partner do not take these feelings personally or feel blamed for your experience.
G. Talking about your feelings can create a better understanding of each other.
H. You choose your feelings based on what you make up as your interpretation of life. People who seem to always be happy have made up a conversation about life that it is all perfect. The gifts and lessons that came with the difficult times were golden!
I. When your partner shares their feelings never say: "You shouldn't feel that way."

They need to have acceptance for however they feel and they need to know you are a safe person and that they can share their feelings with you.

4. Decide what rules you have for disagreeing. Everyone argues. Being each other's protagonists is sometimes challenging, rules can help.

    A. Say what you DO want, not what you don't want, for example: 'Be respectful' instead of no name-calling, 'Create privacy' instead of no fighting in public.

5. Venting to blow off steam.

    A. Warn your partner if you need to vent and let them know they do not need to fix the situation, that you just need to vent about something.

    B. The worst thing you could do when your partner needs to vent is to interrupt them, give them advice, be defensive or justify whatever they are upset about. Your job as a partner is to be their sounding board, just let them hear themselves talk, so they can figure out the issue, even if it is a complaint that involves you. Just listen.

    C. Get out the popcorn when your partner needs to vent. Picture yourself watching some drama unfold in front of you, complete with popcorn. Just watch and listen for the purpose of understanding, not for the purpose of solving, defending or justifying.

D. "I hear you" is a good response.

6. Give each other permission to take a break, go to the cave, think, come back and complete later if you start getting frustrated or angry.

    A. Some people need to think before they talk or respond. Let your partner know when you will be willing to continue talking so they don't think you are just avoiding by running away. Ask for the time you need.

7. Set boundaries before you are angry or after a cool down. People believe that they have to be angry to set boundaries. That comes from how they witnessed boundaries being set as a child. People were usually angry and even threatening. The problem with waiting until you are angry to set boundaries is, that the boundaries you set when you are angry, will only be respected when you are angry. The boundaries that you set when you are calm and peaceful will be respected more often.

But how do I set a boundary?

    A. First determine what you want to say and then say it. You may even want to write it down if boundary setting is new for you.

B. Determine how you are feeling about the situation you want to change.

C. What is happening that you want changed? Don't blame anyone, just state the problem.

D. What do you want to happen instead? You must be specific or it won't happen.

E. Then ask for agreement, just because you state what you want does not mean you are going to get it. Without asking for an agreement, it sounds like a demand.

F. Fill in these blanks to practice:

I feel _____when _____happens,
What I want from you is _____
Would you be willing to _____by
_____?

G. CAUTION: This method of boundary setting only works if you are not blaming. Saying it like this is blaming:

I feel upset when YOU LEAVE THE PLACE A MESS, what I want from you is to clean up YOUR MESS. Would you be willing to clean up after yourself, SO I DON'T HAVE TO DO IT before I get home?

This won't work, it makes your partner feel blamed and wrong but try this instead:

I feel <u>frustrated</u> when <u>the place is a mess when I get home</u>. What I want from you is to <u>clean up after yourself before I get home</u>. Are you willing to <u>clean up your stuff in the living room by 5:30 each night</u>?

If the word "YOU" is used in the second blank it sounds like blaming. You are upset because the place is a mess. It doesn't matter really who made it a mess, does it? So, saying you are upset when the place is a mess is easier for your partner to hear than being blamed for the mess by saying "I am upset when YOU mess the place up."

JOURNAL:
Until you get used to this type of communication write it down in your Journal before you say it. Pick one boundary you would like to set and practice writing out how it would sound now.

---

8. Accepting each other's "Quirks"
We all have Quirks, and we can either choose to nit-pick at each other or we can choose acceptance of our partner like we would like them to accept us.

My mother had lots of quirks. One of them was that she just wasn't happy unless she wasn't happy. She worried about everything and was afraid of mostly everything.

Once my father wanted to surprise her with a gift. He went to his jeweler and said he wanted something very different and classy. He said he had just the thing. He had a Tahitian pearl that was just delivered to him and he was going to set this huge, perfect black pearl in a pendant. My father was very impressed with this luminous pearl and asked him to set it in a platinum setting with a delicate platinum chain.

The day it was ready my father was very excited to bring the gift home. He told my mother to stand in front of the mirror with her eyes closed and he put it around her neck and told her to open her eyes. Her response? "Eww, it looks like a black mole on my chest." My father was crushed. He took it back and had some pave diamonds put on the setting to make it sparkle a little. She later said that it now looked like her mole had a diamond dunce hat on.

She was just not happy unless she was not happy. This "Quirk" of hers devastated my father who always tried to please her.

One day she was complaining about a beautiful new home they had just purchased and my father just shook his head. I said "Dad, she just isn't happy unless she is not happy." She laughed and agreed that was true.

At that moment my father finally accepted that weird personality trait of hers and years of his need to beat himself up for never being good enough floated away. All it took was acceptance of her quirk. They had been married for over 50 years by that point. The last 12 years they had together were much better than the first 50 because he just accepted her quirk.

9. Validate your partner by repeating what you heard them say, you may have misinterpreted and that is a way of clearing up any miscommunication immediately.

We have thousands of filters in our brains that we have formed by making up a conclusion from every experience we have ever had. These filters often become out limiting beliefs. Then we run every new conversation through these skewed filters before we decide our interpretation of that new experience.

Sometimes we make up something that just isn't real because we are applying these filters.

Sometimes we misunderstand people because we are expecting them to add evidence to what we already believe. When you see someone react to a conversation in a way that does not match with the intention of what was being said, it is sometimes helpful to say, "What did you hear me say?"

If they misinterpreted the conversation, there is time to correct their assumption before a misunderstanding can destroy a relationship.

In order to make sure we are hearing what our partner wanted us to hear, try repeating back to them exactly what you heard them say.

My husband is the cook in the house and he is very possessive of all of his pots and pans and cooking gadgets.

One day I was attempting to cook an egg. He was behind me watching my every move, which I found very annoying. Then he pointed to a tiny silver dot on his Teflon pan and said: "Do you know how that got there? SOMEONE used a metal instrument on it." I started fuming so he quickly said: "Oh, what did you hear me say?" Now I am half fuming and half laughing, and I said: "I heard you say you love your no stick frying pan more than you love ME!" We both laughed but the phrase "What did you hear me say?" worked and defused the situation.

In more serious situations I have seen this phrase be really necessary to get to the bottom of something that lies hidden. I know a couple where he was badly hurt and disappointed by a woman when he was very young.

Now the filter that he has regarding love is one that tells him "Anyone who you love can and will hurt you." Or "You will disappoint anyone that you allow to love you." Every time any woman tells him that she loves him he runs that through his filter of fear and rejects it, or resents it, or just plain runs away. If someone would just ask him, "What did you hear me say?" he may discover all the underlying conversations that he has that are preventing him from fully experiencing love.

> What he might be hearing women say when they say "I love you," is this:
> I will demand you give up your freedom
> I will hurt you
> I will be disappointed by you
> I will make demands of you
> I will try to control you
> I will cheat on you
> I will leave you
> I will smother you
> I will trap you

The words "I love you" don't mean anything unless you say they do. You are making it all up; you are the author.

Maybe if he could actually hear these beliefs that are in his head they would no longer destroy his chance of giving and receiving love. If he realized he was in control and no one could do these things to him without his permission maybe he wouldn't be so afraid.

You are also in control of setting any boundaries you need to in order to feel safe to love and be loved.

Awareness is the key, and a simple way to start discovering what your filters are and where they came from is the question "What did you hear me say?" when your partner's reaction seems inappropriate.

Now if you want a huge disconnect or an argument make sure to say "You are over-reacting" instead.

10. Accept advice or suggestions from your protagonist. Sometimes we don't want to listen to our partner, we hear them all the time, and we discount their advice or suggestions.

Try this experiment. Read this bit of advice and close your eyes and think about how you feel about this advice and just think of it as information:

"You need to take better care of yourself."

How do you feel about this?

Now read this bit of advice and close your eyes and think about how you feel about this advice, but this time think of it as urgent and important information:

"You need to take better care of yourself."

Now how do you feel about this?

Now read this bit of advice and close your eyes and think about how you feel about this advice, but now think of this as a clear message from God:

"You need to take better care of yourself."

Now how do you feel about the information?

We can't always hear God speak to us or our loved ones who have passed on before us, but if they want to get a message to us, they may speak to you through the ones who love you.

Do your best to listen to your partner with new ears, like what they say matters, and it may be a message.

11. WATCH YOUR TONE OF VOICE! Most arguments, up to 90%, stem from the tone of voice being used, not the content of what is being said!

A tone of voice that is impatient, angry or condescending can trigger all kinds of past experiences. Then we tend to make each other pay for other people's mistakes.

Choose a tone of voice and a 'way of being' that creates closeness instead of distance. There is no such thing as "This is just the way I am." We CHOOSE our way of being. We are all like a chameleon, able to shift into 1000 different ways of being.

I own all ways of being, so I can adapt and still be the real me. Some are comfortable and some are "new," but all are available to you.

WHAT DID YOU HEAR ME SAY?

Chapter 9.

TAKE 100% RESPONSIBILITY FOR EVERYTHING!

Often people's concept of "Responsibility" is all about blame and fault, guilt, duty, burden and obligation. What if I told you that responsibility was freedom and enlightenment and growth and control?

Let's look at what Responsibility is NOT and then we can see what it is.

A. Blame is looking for a scapegoat, someone to lay the mistake on, someone to point at as being the cause of the error. This takes all cause for admonishment away from us and delivers it to them.

B. Fault is the cause of the blunder, the source of the mistake. "It's my fault" is self-blame but has no real responsibility attached to it.

C. Duty is something that is expected of you. You may choose to do what you believe is your "duty" but duty implies that whether you choose it or not you MUST do it.

D. Burden is something you would never choose, it has been inflicted upon you by someone or some circumstance but your free will does not create it.

E. Obligation is something you believe you owe someone else. You choose it because it is what you believe to be right and ethical.

Are these the thoughts that run through your head when you hear the word "Responsibility? There is no value in Responsibility if that is the way you have it wired. That conversation you have in your head about responsibility can have you run from it, shirk it, see it as a way to open yourself to criticism and judgement. But that is not the TRUTH, it is just your belief. If your belief is causing you grief, make up a new one. YOU are the author of everything you believe. What if instead you saw responsibility as a joy, the greatest gift in life? What if it was the one ingredient that brought you freedom, growth, enlightenment, and control? What if it was the necessary element for love?

A. Freedom is experienced when you are the creator of your life and your experience. The only way to truly be the Captain of your own ship is to be 100% responsible for the ups and downs of the voyage. Navigating the lessons of the sea and adjusting the sails to have a more safe, pleasant cruise as you go.

B. Enlightenment happens when you learn from your experiences. When you are learning lessons, everything is worth it. Every event is valuable.

C. Growth happens when you are forced to get uncomfortable and stretch so that every experience broadens your horizons and removes the fear of the unknown. With growth comes courage to go further next time.

D. Control is so important to so many of us who have not yet discovered that it is just an illusion. None of us are really in control. We set up our lives in predictable rituals to make us feel in control. The fact is that a million things can knock us off that script. The only real control is in our mind. It is what we make up as our interpretation of every single experience. That is what we have control of only.

RESPONSIBIITY IS A CONVERSATION WE HAVE WITH OURSELVES

E. Love is the result of taking 100% responsibility for everything. If you are blaming someone or holding them accountable in any way for your lot in life then loving them is difficult if not impossible. The only way we can experience unconditional love is to take 100% responsibility for our life and experiences.

Remember, loving someone unconditionally does NOT mean supporting them unconditionally. I can love someone unconditionally but only support what is healthy, loving and functional. We all have that choice.

Often people will refer back to the old paradigm that a relationship is 50/50. That will give you a half-baked relationship, no one willing to take ownership. A healthy, loving and functional relationship is 100%/100%. But who takes responsibility first? YOU do. It is a very powerful and attractive process to witness and it is contagious.

Often when people are a witness to someone taking responsibility it is so powerful that they want to look at their own responsibility too.

But HOW do we go through the process of taking 100% responsibility? We need to ask ourselves some questions and search for answers that will empower us, enlighten us and bring us gratitude rather than interpretations that would beat us or others up with guilt, blame and shame.

Anger, the need for forgiveness or the need to apologize totally evaporate when sharing the process of taking responsibility! These are what I call the "Miracle Questions."

First of all, establish exactly what it is that needs to be addressed. I am taking 100% responsibility for ruining our date (insert whatever fits here, marriage, vacation, finances, whatever).

Then ask yourself "How did I create it?" Be honest with yourself. I created it by being distracted, impatient and withholding. I created it by not asking for what I wanted. I created it by being too focused on work instead of us. I created it by being worried about money, the kids, whatever. If you are not sure how you created the breakdown, just ask yourself what would I do differently if I had it to do over. That may help you figure out what you did to create the situation.

Next, ask yourself what the gifts and lessons are that you are learning from this. There are always gifts and lessons. For example: I am learning that unless I am present and in a loving space going out on a date is not a good idea. I am learning that all I really needed to do was vent to you about my day, and I could have been free to focus on us. I am learning that maybe a 15-minute meditation before a date to visualize what I want to create with you would be valuable. The gift is that we can make another date and I can use everything I learned tonight to make it great.

The last part is just proclaiming what is going to be different on future dates. This is what I could have done differently. This is what I will do from now on.

"I could have told you what was going on with me before we went out. In the future I will get myself calm and focused before we go out on a date so we can enjoy ourselves."

Being the recipient of that process is way better than an apology because "I'm sorry" does not indicate that you know what caused the breakdown, or that you learned anything or that anything will be different in the future. There are people who need to hear the "I'm sorry" but say that after you have explained your responsibility process to them.

JOURNAL:
All the things that I have blamed my partner for in the past that I can now take responsibility for are:

JOURNAL:

Now list each thing that you blamed your partner for and apply these questions to each one. Journal your answers.

HERE ARE THE MIRACLE QUESTIONS TO ASK YOURSELF:

First, establish what it is exactly for which you are taking responsibility. Now answer these questions:

1. How did I create it?
2. What are the gifts and lessons?
3. What is going to be different now that I am aware?

VERBALIZING RESPONSIBILITY:

This is what I am taking responsibility for…
(NOT "This is my part in it" true responsibility is 100% ownership)
1. This is how I created it.
2. This is what I learned, the gifts & lessons.
3. This is what I will do differently in the future.

So here are a few examples of couples who have used the tool of Responsibility to save or transform their relationships.

Couple A:
A high-powered successful attorney and his yoga loving wife had a breakdown when the wife found out he cheated. They came to me with the desire to figure out a way to get beyond this and keep the marriage together.

The husband was a bit of a sex addict, he wanted and needed sex frequently and his wife knew this and also enjoyed the frequency and intensity of their sex life.

She was very into yoga and decided to become a yoga instructor which meant she had to go away for several weeks over a year. Her husband didn't seem to mind at first but he grew cranky and tired of his wife being away so much. One night when she was gone he went to a strip club and brought home a willing participant. When his wife returned she found a cheap earring under her pillow. All hell broke loose. He had to tell the truth.

Here is how he took responsibility:
1. How he created it? He knew his wife's absence was becoming a problem but instead of talking about it and looking for a solution he acted out of resentment.

2. What did he learn? He learned that if he is willing to be open and vulnerable and honest and to communicate his feelings that they can find a solution together.
3. What was going to be different? In the future they would talk before any trips and decide if he wanted to go with her or if he was OK home alone.

He actually became certified as a yoga instructor too and when he retired they enjoyed traveling around the country putting on weekend yoga retreats. When people ask him how he got involved in yoga, he and his wife just say, long story. He never cheated again but they also helped several other couples who had the experience of infidelity save their marriages by sharing their story of responsibility.

Here is how she took responsibility:
1. How she created it? She knew that her husband was feeling neglected but she was afraid if they talked about it that he would ask her to stop pursuing her dream so she pretended not to know and even stayed away from creating a lot of closeness when she was there for fear that he would say something about being lonely and feeling undesirable.
2. What did she learn? A lot of pain could have been avoided with communicating feelings and desires and that she should have trusted her intuition.

3. What was going to be different? In the future she was going to trust her intuition and be brave enough to talk about what might be uncomfortable so that she was creating closeness instead of distance.

Now many people may be saying right now, Oh, NO! If he cheats, he is gone! Well, I'm sure that may be true for many people, but for others, it is not a 'deal breaker,' and there could be tremendous gifts and lessons in every situation that you are willing to work through and use the tool of 100% responsibility to get through it. Remember, we started this book by saying that every relationship is like a fingerprint.

Couple B:
A couple in their 30's who had two children and lived in a 'vacation town' where there was a lot of partying. The woman was a bit of a workaholic and the man was a homebody but liked to be in the outdoors. He had a drinking problem. His wife started to realize it when there was always some drama that occurred when he drank. She asked him to stop drinking, but it got worse and so did the dramas, injuries, arrests and hospitals. The escalation of drama and chaos was more than his wife could tolerate. Finally, she left and told him he had two weeks to decide if he wanted his family or alcohol, but he could not have both. He chose his family.

Here is how he took responsibility:
1. How he created it: He knew he drank too much and he did nothing to get help or stop himself. His excess escalated until there were huge, dangerous and expensive breakdowns that affected his entire family, including the children.
2. What he learned: Alcohol was like poison to him and if he wanted his family and if he wanted a healthy, loving and functional life it could not include alcohol, ever.
3. What was going to be different: It was understood that he physically could not manage the effects of alcohol on his body and he chose to be alcohol free so that he could have the life and family of his dreams.

Here is how she took responsibility:
1. How she created it: She met him in a bar. She was well aware that he drank too much but she was way too busy to deal with his drinking and she never wanted to upset the applecart so she pretended it was no big deal until she was dealing with way too much drama.
2. What she learned: Tell the truth and tell it fast, don't avoid dealing with problems or they will escalate.
3. What was going to be different? She would take a stand, even if it were uncomfortable.

Couple C:
Middle aged couple who were hard working and both had their own businesses. Let's call them Chris and Pat. So, Chris was kind of a workaholic and not very domestic, but Chris handled the money. Pat preferred to not make decisions for fear of being held responsible for a bad outcome so Pat delegated most decisions to Chris. They decided to make some Real Estate investments because values were going through the roof and Chris thought it would be a good retirement strategy. Pat agreed. Well, the Real Estate market crashed and they lost everything. Pat blamed Chris for the financial breakdown.

How Chris took responsibility:
1. How Chris created it: Chris was very controlling and was the designer of the entire plan. Pat was barely consulted because Chris didn't want to hear the plan analyzed to death. Pat's input would have at least slowed things down, but Pat wasn't asked.
2. What Chris learned: Even when you think you are absolutely sure of your plan it is always good to get other input from your partner.
3. What was going to be different: Even if things took longer and even if it was frustrating to Chris to wait before taking action, Chris was now going to ask for Pat's opinion, ideas and feedback before making a decision. That would be more like a partnership!

How Pat took responsibility:
1. **How did Pat create it: Pat's intuition said: "The Real Estate market is not safe right now." Pat did not say anything to Chris and instead just agreed so there would be no conflict.**
2. **What did Pat learn: Pat's opinion and intuition are valuable and withholding that from your partner causes problems worse than the conflict that can be caused by hashing it out.**
3. **What would be different: Pat decided not to agree on anything before expressing opinions, communicating intuition and feeling heard.**

JOURNAL:

How I feel when I blame my partner is:

How I feel when I take responsibility is:

There was a story about two twin boys who were very different. One was a pessimist and the other an optimist.

At Christmas the parents did an experiment. They put the pessimist in a room with a beautifully decorated tree and dozens of brightly wrapped gifts. They put the optimist in a room with a bare tree and a pile of horse manure.

They went back to the first room, and the pessimist had opened all his gifts, and he looked up at them and said "Is that all there is?" Then they went to the next room, and the optimist was gleefully digging through the manure. The parents said, "What on earth are you doing?" The optimist answered, "I know there is a pony in here somewhere!"

Moral of the story, when looking for the gifts and lessons in order to take responsibility, keep digging, there is a pony in there somewhere.

IT IS WHAT YOU SAY IT IS

Chapter 10.

DO YOU WANT TO BE RIGHT OR BE HAPPY?

There are four priorities that the ego has: being comfortable, being in control, being approved of and being RIGHT. All of these priorities can devastate a relationship but none worse than the need to be right.

One of the beliefs that people have that create all kinds of conflict in a relationship is the belief that your partner must agree with you on everything. Arguments ensue when one person insists on convincing their partner that they are wrong and the partner is right. They believe that their partner must concede, by the end of the argument, that they are wrong and they must agree with their partner. Why? Who said?

Our job is to communicate what we believe and why, so that our partner understands us, they don't need to agree with us, they just need to understand. We can all just agree to disagree. It is not your job to convince your partner that you are right. It is your job to explain yourself so that you are understood. It is your job also to understand your partner.

I was raised Roman Catholic. I enjoyed going to mass and I explained the teachings of the Catholic Church to my husband and let him know what I believed.

He is an agnostic, a naturist. He was never baptized, had no formal religion but was raised to see God in nature.

Neither of us attempted to convert the other, but we sure did share a lot about our spiritual beliefs. We appreciate each other's beliefs and how we came to embrace them. We understand each other. There is no need for agreement; there is only a need for understanding. We model all of our different beliefs after how we handled our differences in spirituality.

Neither of us needed to be right. We choose to be close instead. We choose to be happy instead. We choose love instead.

JOURNAL:

What am I trying to be right about?
When would I rather be right than be happy?
When would I rather be right than be close?
When would I rather be right than be peaceful?

JOURNAL:

Look at some of the beliefs that you made up based on your past experiences, to see what has created your "filters" that you may be making your partner pay for. Fill in the blanks:

Men are _____
I made this belief up based on this past experience:

_____

Women
are_____
I made this belief up based on this past experience:

_____

Relationships
are_____
I made this belief up based on this past experience:

_____

My partner
always_____
I made this belief up based on this past experience:

_____

My partner
never_____
I made this belief up based on this past experience:

_____

This need to be right is getting in my way of being happy. I am now "willing to be wrong" about these beliefs in order to create what I really want.

There are four priorities that the ego has: being right, being approved of, being in control and being COMFORTABLE. All of these priorities can devastate a relationship but none are more subtle destroyers than the need to be comfortable.

I knew a couple who were together for over 20 years and everything seemed great in their marriage as far as she was concerned. One day her partner came home and said "I'm leaving you." She was floored, shocked and devastated. "What is wrong?" she said, "Why?" He said "I'm bored." She asked "Is there someone else?" he admitted there was. "Who is it?" she demanded. "My office manager" he revealed.

"What?" she shouted. "That woman who you come home complaining about every day?" "Yes, her" he answered. "But why?" she pleaded. "She challenges me" was his response.

They had gotten comfortable, they stopped being each other's protagonists. She used to ask him to go dancing and he said he would rather watch TV. He used to ask her to go bowling and she said she would rather not, so bowling night turned into office manager night. They sank into the most comfortable, non-challenging life possible. There was little spark left, and even sex was like trying to light a wet ash as they didn't want to get uncomfortable there either.

JOURNAL:

If I were willing to get uncomfortable in my relationship these are the things I would talk about:
If I were willing to get uncomfortable in my relationship these are the things I would do:
If I were willing to get uncomfortable in my relationship these are the places I would go:
If I were willing to get uncomfortable in my relationship these are the things I would experiment with:
If I were willing to get uncomfortable in my relationship these are the things I would ask my partner to do:

There are four priorities that the ego has: being comfortable, being right, being approved of and being in CONTROL. All of these priorities can devastate a relationship, but none are more abusive destroyers than the need to be in control.

First of all, control is an illusion; no one really has total control. They may have an ability to manipulate and intimidate others into not challenging them. They may have a regiment that seems like they are in control, but at any moment something can happen that knocks them right off their horse.

When we attempt to control others, we tend to be abusive. If our demands and expectations are not met the controlling style personality may use some emotional abuse or blackmail to get their way. They may just use a tone of voice that warns their partner that if they don't want a big fight they better just let their partner have their way.

The person whose priority is control needs to practice letting their partner decide and plan things and do things their way. They need to practice flexibility and patience. The "My way or the Highway" mode of doing relationship is lethal.

I am a controlling style personality. Once I ran into an old friend, and we talked for a while at a restaurant. After about a half an hour he asked me a question that changed my life.

He said "Tina, what would your life be like if you gave up some of that control?" My initial response was I wanted to smack him. How dare he challenge my need for control! That question bothered me so much I knew he was right.

I started using that question as a mantra, and I meditated on it. I applied it to every area of my life and I asked myself over and over again for months, "What would my life be like if I gave up some of that control?"

In my Career, I realized that I could train other people to take over for me and let them lead. Then I found freedom.

Looking at how giving up control would affect my self-care I realized that it would enable me to do all the things I was avoiding, losing weight, ending bad habits and starting healthy ones.

When I looked at how my need for control kept me from being the biggest contribution I could be, I realized that it just doesn't need to look exactly like I think it does. I ended up being a political activist with over five hundred thousand followers.

The biggest difference that question made was when I applied it to all my relationships. That was the most challenging area to give up control, but it was also the most necessary. It improved my relationships with my adult children, my husband, and others.

You can imagine their relief when instead of wanting to engineer everything I just started listening to what they wanted, told them I believed in them, and I was here if they wanted any support. Period. If I had suggestions, I would ask permission instead of saying "You SHOULD do this…. or that."

There are four priorities that the ego has: being in control, being right, being comfortable and being APPROVED OF. All of these priorities can devastate a relationship but none are more deep-seated destroyers than the need to be approved of, or to "look good" to others.

The need to impress others steals our authenticity. If we are not genuine in our relationships it is impossible to be intimate. Remember intimacy is all about "IN-TO-ME-SEE." If "looking good" is your motivation then you are unwilling to take risks, it is a fear-based motivation. You are afraid of being judged instead of just being real and honest. To get over this ask your partner for acceptance.

JOURNAL:

WHAT IS LOVE? Write down all over one journal page scattered words that describe what you believe LOVE is. When you are complete, then continue reading.

Chapter 11.

LOVE

WHAT IS LOVE?

Love is not something that just happens to you. LOVE IS A CHOICE, at first an unconscious one, maybe, like the concept of "falling" in love. At first, love may be a choice based on feelings; feelings of connection, feelings of fulfillment of an emptiness or a distant feeling of familiarity that might be seen as fate or destiny as in the "soul mate" theory. Eventually though, the choice of love, becomes more conscious. Even in the times when you don't "feel" love, you can still "choose" love. The opposite of love is not hatred; it is fear. When choosing to love we become vulnerable. We know that even though we may get hurt, we can still choose Love!

WHO ARE WE MAKING PAY FOR PAST EXPERIENCES?

Sometimes we make the people in our life pay the prices for what others did in our past. Realizing what you are doing and why can help you be present and in the moment with your partner. The next exercise was inspired by something called an IMAGO which was developed by Harville Hendrix who has written some great relationship books. This will show you what you may have been making your partner pay for and who it was who helped you develop those filters and walls.

LOVE IS A CHOICE

JOURNAL: Part I
~ Skip a few spaces between each answer ~

Name three positive traits of any parent or caregiver that you remember as a child.

Name three negative traits of any parent or caregiver that you remember as a child.

Name feelings you experienced during positive childhood memories.

Name any actions you took in response to childhood negativity.

JOURNAL: PART II.

Above the answers you wrote to the questions in Part I please write these new headings:

~~Name three positive traits of any parent or caregiver that you remember as a child.~~
I am trying to reproduce these traits in my partner:

~~Name three negative traits of any parent or caregiver that you remember as a child.~~
These are the traits I am comfortable with, looking for or willing to accept:

~~Name feelings you experienced during positive childhood memories.~~
I'm trying to experience these feelings:

~~Name any actions you took in response to childhood negativity.~~
I stop myself from getting this sometimes by:

Now read back the new headings and the answers under them. Can you see now how you may be making your partner pay for your past? Can you see how you may have formed some unhealthy filters and some limiting beliefs about relationships? Can you see what you could do differently that may improve your relationship?

When you think about how we choose a partner, it makes sense. Let's face it; everyone has some negative characteristics. Even someone nearly perfect has 'being a perfectionist' as an annoying characteristic.

So, in our human need to "be comfortable" we would gravitate towards people who had the same negative traits as the ones we already knew how to deal with. This is why often people wake up one day and say, "Oh God! I married my mother!" or my father.

The same issues will keep surfacing in our lives and our relationships until we learn the gifts and lessons we are supposed to on our Journey to US: Unique Solutions.

If our parent was an alcoholic, and we swore we would never turn into an alcoholic, but we end up in a relationship with an alcoholic, it is because there is some lesson to learn, some gift to receive, some oneness to accept.

In our divine wisdom, we will continue to choose people with addiction issues until we figure out what it is we are supposed to learn. Keep digging, once you learned the lesson the universe will set you free to choose someone with another issue to be your teacher. Trust the process.

Chapter 12.

COMMITMENT VS FEELINGS

The purpose of commitment is to forward our lives and our relationships with a vision, a direction, and a partner. Feelings are more like instincts or emotions that lead us based on comfort, drama, fear, ego or the easy way out, but our commitment will always take us on the road less traveled, and to higher ground.

If we act based on our feelings we may stay in bed all day, eat everything in sight, cheat on our partner and beat our kids but if we choose out of our commitment to our partner, our home, our health, our family, etc. we act with integrity, staying true to our intention of what we want to create.

Commitment is a guide, a pledge. Your results are just your feedback as to what you are really committed to as intention often equals results. Often people will say "this just happened, it was not my intention." Based on results it absolutely was your intention.

If you live a life of responsibility you will not see yourself as a victim of circumstances, you will see how you have been the creator of everything.

Taking 100% responsibility for everything is a much more powerful way to live and you will create way more of the results that you intend to if you live with the paradigm that "Based on results, I must have intended this, because this is what I have." Then you can look for the payoffs of having that result that you claim you didn't intend to see why, maybe, you did.

If you start a conflict with your spouse then storm out to a bar and sit wallowing in your victim story as you hang out with friends and drink then you may want to look at the payoff to fighting with your partner as "When we fight I then get to have a great excuse to go out, meet friends and drink." Wow.

The payoffs to not created what you claim were the intended results are that you then have excuses to do things that you may not normally do.

Let's look at an example. Someone who has an unintended pregnancy can say this was not my intention or they can say based on results I must have intended to get pregnant. Then you can look at the gifts and lessons of the pregnancy based on possibility instead of fear and resentment.

There are prices and payoffs for every decision you make especially in relationships. If you decide to have sex you have a load of risks and consequences that go along with that. Only one of which is pregnancy.

Most people have an emotional reaction to having sex. They feel closer to the person after having an intimate sexual experience and often they want 'more' from that person afterwards. They want "what's next."

What does that mean? It is different for everyone, they want a date, a dinner, a ring, a marriage, more sex, a house, a baby. This is an example of seeing how your results often equal your intention as allowing yourself to get close enough to someone to have sex opens the door to "what's next."

Based on results, that must have been what you wanted. If you live intentionally you will think of the possible consequences of your actions before you act. Those actions will be based on your commitment to your vision for your life not your feelings.

Story #3: Commitment vs Feelings

Only people in the military can understand what a military family's challenges are. A couple who had both been in the military shared this story with me.

After several relatively uneventful deployments to Iraq and Afghanistan over a long career in the military there was one that turned out to be life altering. The Airman was off duty but not in his quarters, his bunkmate was.

The trailer where they stayed was blown up by some ragtag bunch of rebels. The Airman's bunkmate was killed.

This trauma of knowing that if he had made one different decision, that would have led him to his trailer, he would have been dead too, changed the way he thought about life. He started to adapt the "nothing matters" attitude and "Life is so short, just do whatever you 'feel' like doing" philosophy.

This did not support his marriage and the commitment he made to his wife and family. His wife, having spent several years in the same branch of the military also, understood exactly what was happening. Her level of commitment, no matter how she was feeling about his actions, was at 100%. She held the family together until they could work through the feelings her husband was having. Sometimes it just takes one to remember the commitment! They are doing great now!

You may not always feel love. You may not always experience the emotion of 'being in love' but you can always choose love.

Feelings of love might be compassion, kindness, closeness or affection and we may experience these feelings sometimes but not always.

Emotions of being in love may be romance, passion, fascination, infatuation, and we may experience these emotions sometimes but not always.

Loving actions include being helpful, listening, being affectionate, being intimate, being grateful and being communicative. These are choices and are always possible no matter how you feel or no matter what emotions you are experiencing.

JOURNAL:

Write down all the feelings of love that you may have.
Write down all the emotions of being in love you have ever experienced.
Write down all the ways that to can choose love.

What are feelings good for? If we need to take actions based on our commitment instead of our feelings then what are feelings good for?

If you share feelings you can create intimacy and understanding: (IN-TO-ME-SEE)

The worst thing you could possibly do is to tell your partner that they "shouldn't feel that way" or to take their feelings personally.

No one makes you feel anything, you choose your feelings based on your interpretation of events, based on your thousands of filters from the past or hopefully based on intentional living.

Decide whether you want to create closeness or distance, then choose how you want to feel. What feelings would support that intention, then choose that. You may not believe that you have that much control, but you do and with practice you can be the master of your emotions.

No one makes you or your partner feel anything either. Feelings are not right or wrong, they are not good or bad, you have an interpretation of which feelings are positive or negative, and you may share or withhold your feelings based on that judgement. What if you believed that feelings are not right or wrong, not good or bad? Your feelings are just indicators of what you need to pay attention to.

WHY DO WE FEAR FEELINGS?

What feelings would create low or negative energy? Worry, dread, anger, blame, fear, resentment, shame, guilt, etc. These are feelings you may not want to share but how could sharing them be valuable? It may give your partner some insight about you or some understanding or compassion. All feelings are valuable to share but not to act upon. The goal is not to change how your partner feels, it is just to understand how they feel.

What feelings would create high or positive energy? Love, joy, reverence, awe, appreciation, laughter, peace, gratitude, etc. These are the feelings when shared bring us closer together and give us a stronger connection.

JOURNAL:

What feelings do I judge as bad or wrong?
What feelings do I judge as good or right?
If I were not afraid what feelings would I share?
What feelings do I need to make sure I do not act upon?

Chapter 13

HEALING.

Healing. This is a huge subject that 1,000 books could be written on because it is such a personal Journey, no two experiences can be exactly alike.

First, we need to know that it is said that no one can love beyond their own experience of being loved as a child. For people who do not work on themselves that may be true, but for those who really want something different than what they have already experienced, they are willing to learn and grow and get uncomfortable. We need to be a safe place for each other to look at our past, not as a victim story, but as a plethora of possible gifts and lessons to help each other discover and sort out. That takes being willing to be honest and vulnerable and making an agreement to be there for each other WITHOUT judgement.

When we offer each other the five elements necessary to create a healthy, loving and functional relationship, we make this kind of intimate communication safer.

Learning how to give and receive what we call the FIVE "A"s; Attention, affection, acceptance, approval and acknowledgement is paramount in the process of healing.

We are going to explore our relationship with these five principles of a healthy, loving and functional relationship but first, we should look at the prices we have paid for missing some of these essential elements; addictions.

We are all addicted to something:
Sex, drugs, alcohol, shopping, gambling, worry, pornography, smoking, sports, binging, sweets, credit cards, television, collecting, hoarding, nail-biting, cutting, shoes, clubbing, fanaticism, love, criticism, purses, drama, judgment, work, food, education, analyzing, cleaning, the gym, grooming, impetuousness, blurting, sleeping, soap operas, surgery, internet, organization, religion, pets, books, paper piling, etc.

All these different compulsions, obsessions and addictions that are the result of missing a part or all of these 5 "A"s:

Attention
Affection
Acceptance
Approval
Acknowledgement

If you did not receive these essential elements of development as a child, then you were damaged and have some "holes in your bucket" that you have been attempting to fill with one of the above addictions to make you "feel" good.

JOURNAL:

What is your favorite way to fill your bucket? Sex, drugs, alcohol, shopping, gambling, worry, pornography, smoking, sports, binging, sweets, credit cards, television, collecting, hoarding, nail-biting, cutting, shoes, clubbing, fanaticism, love, criticism, purses, drama, judgment, work, food, education, analyzing, cleaning, the gym, grooming, impetuousness, blurting, sleeping, soap operas, surgery, internet, organization, religion, pets, books, paper piling, or another addictive behavior?

What does it mean?
EG: I smoked for years. What it meant for me was that I had freedom, I was in control, and I was like my mother.

My partner was a hoarder, what it meant was that he retained a connection with the people who had died who previously owned the objects of his affection.

How does it make you feel?
EG: Smoking made me feel powerful and in control.
Hoarding made my partner feel loved and connected.

What need did it satisfy? Attention, Affection, Acceptance, Approval or Acknowledgement?

EG: Smoking filled my need to be the captain of my own ship. (Acceptance).
Hoarding filled a need to avoid loss and grief. (Affection)

JOURNAL:
Go to each addictive behavior you listed and now answer these questions about each one:
What does it mean?
How does it make you feel?
What need did it satisfy? Attention, Affection, Acceptance, Approval or Acknowledgement?

What every child needs to become a healthy loving functional adult is the same as what every partner needs to deliver to create a healthy, loving, functional relationship. These elements are easy to deliver and when you are aware which ones your partner needs most you can look for ways to deliver them.

Let's look at each need to define what they really mean.

ATTENTION:

ATTENTION consists of quality time together, creating relationship, sharing knowledge with each other, being open, revealing, being vulnerable, conversation, intimacy (IN-TO-ME-SEE)

If you were not given the attention you craved and deserved as a child you were treated with ABSENCE, you may have been ignored or even a latch key kid. This treatment would have made a hole in your bucket.

The way to repair that hole is AWARENESS, to pay attention to yourself via personal growth, self-awareness, reading, meditation and reflection on your life for the purpose of being the best YOU that you can be. (MENTAL stimulation, quality time).

AFFECTION:

AFFECTION is any physical expressions of love, kindness or compassion. Affection is the expression of love using the five senses especially touch. This would include massages, hugs, sex, eye contact, sharing music, art, fragrance, anything that would please your five senses.

The lack of affection would have been ALOOFNESS, where the people who were supposed to show you love were cold, distant, awkward with physical affection, detached, maybe even physically abusive instead. Receiving no physical touch, having senses deprived or having shame attached to touch would result in another hole in your emotional bucket.

The way to repair this hole is to give yourself physical love, AMORE. That means to treat your body the best that you can with massage, healthy food, vitamins, baths, exercise, all the physical care you can give yourself. (PHYSICAL love, touch).

ACCEPTANCE:

ACCEPTANCE is the most challenging of the five "A"s as it usually requires people to alter their own beliefs. Acceptance of your partner's opinions, differing beliefs, personality traits, mistakes, quirks, failures, weaknesses and strengths is what is needed to deliver this need.

If you did not receive acceptance growing up then you would have received some level of ABUSE such as punishment for making mistakes or not surrendering to someone else's beliefs or wishes, that would bore another hole in your bucket.

The way to repair this hole is through ACCOUNTABILITY. Instead of blaming yourself and finding yourself at fault you can instead take on the exciting adventure of taking 100% responsibility for everything, be accountable. Make it your mission to search for the gifts and lessons in every experience until you find them. (GROWTH through learning) Remember, there is a pony in there somewhere, keep digging!

APPROVAL:

APPROVAL of a loved one's results or efforts, dreams, goals, accomplishments, choices or decisions is the kind of "Good job" pat on the back that people need to experience pride and self-esteem, knowing that the most important people in their life see that they are doing something that is valuable. Approval can also be shown with gifts to memorialize an achievement, a card, or something tangible that will be a celebration and a reminder of their accomplishment.

If we were not given the approval that we needed then we may have experienced ABANDONMENT instead. We may have been disappointing, disowned, dismissed or even looked at with disgust and disapproval. Negative feedback may be the only thing that is remembered and that would drill huge holes in our buckets.

In order to repair that hole what we need is gratitude or APPRECIATION. We need to pat ourselves on the back for creating the life we have. Write a list of everything you are grateful for. I start every morning being grateful for a shower. I have hot running water, I have fragrant bath gels and I have a shower head that is awesome and a wand that comes free. Being grateful for my shower starts my day with gratitude. (SPIRITUAL connection)

ACKNOWLEDGEMENT:

ACKNOWLEDGEMENT consists of verbal compliments of character, talent, abilities and personality. This is a way to say "I SEE YOU" with words of affirmation. This is not about results, this is about character.

If we did not ever hear acknowledgement what we probably remember is ASSESSMENT or judgement of who we were. That would make holes in our bucket too. So, if we did not receive these five "A" the way to repair this hole is very simple, give yourself words of AFFIRMATION every day. Even if you do not believe them at first, fake it till you make it, tell yourself every day that you have three traits or characteristics that you admire in other. (EMOTIONAL, self-nurturing)

For example, write in your mirror every morning "I am a _____, _____, _____ and fill in the blanks with such affirmations like I am worthy, attractive, intelligent, or I am honest, courageous and kind. Whatever you know you need to remind yourself about who you are in order to have a good day and be willing to create closeness with your partner.

So these are the 5 "A"s that we need to give and receive in order to have a healthy, loving functional relationship.

Attention
Affection
Acceptance
Approval
Acknowledgement

What we experienced instead of the five "A"s that has damaged our emotional bucket and contributed to our dysfunctional relationships. This is what made those holes in our buckets that make us always feeling like there is never enough of whatever we are looking for.

Absence
Aloofness
Abuse
Abandonment
Assessment

Only we can repair those holes in our bucket. Here's how:

Awareness
Amore
Accountability
Appreciation
Affirmation

JOURNAL:

Giving and receiving each one of the "5 A's" is imperative to a healthy, loving, functional, committed, adult relationship. Journal where you experience each one of the five "A"s in your life now?

Attention _____

Affection _____

Acceptance _____

Approval _____

Acknowledgement _____

Next: Where do you experience the opposite of the 5 A's in your life now? These experiences may be making the hole in the bucket grow ever larger and make it more difficult to ever feel satisfied. That lack of fulfillment will have us continue to search outside of us to fill the leaking bucket which can damage a relationship.

Absence _____

Aloofness _____

Abuse _____

Abandonment _____

Assessment _____

Sometimes we received the five "A"s from one parent and not the other, sometimes we didn't receive them from either parent, sometimes all were missing or just some were but there are consequences to having those holes in our emotional buckets. No matter how much love we receive now as adults it seems to just run out of the holes in our buckets and leave us looking for love in all the wrong places. But have faith, the holes can be repaired but only WE can repair our own damaged buckets.

JOURNAL:

How do I plan to give the 5 "A"s to my partner?

Attention_____

Affection_____

Acceptance_____

Approval_____

Acknowledgement_____

How do I want my partner to give me the 5 "A"s?

Attention_____

Affection_____

Acceptance_____

Approval_____

Acknowledgement_____

REPAIRING THE HOLES

First, we need to look at why this is important. To make a relationship the very best it can be you must make working on yourself a priority. My first book "The Journey to YOU, more than a book, an experience" is a great way to do some work on yourself so that you are bringing the best YOU possible to any relationship.

Let's look at how we sometimes are drawn to things outside of ourselves to fill our bucket.

When we take a drink why do we do it? When we buy something we don't need, what are we trying to FEEL? Here are all the things we do to attempt to fill the leaky bucket full of holes:

ADDICTIONS, OBSESSIONS & COMPULSIONS (AOC)

Sex, drugs, alcohol, shopping, gambling, worry, pornography, smoking, sports, binging, sweets, credit cards, television, collecting, hoarding, nail biting, cutting, shoes, clubbing, fanaticism, love, criticism, purses, drama, judgment, work, food, education, analyzing, cleaning, the gym, grooming, impetuousness, blurting, sleeping, soap operas, surgery, internet, organization, religion, pets, books, paper piling, etc.

Which of these experiences or activities do you use to "feel" something or to avoid feeling something? Let's look at which activities you choose to fill your bucket now as an adult.

The reason these activities end up turning into addictions, obsessions and compulsions is because no matter how much healthy, loving functional experiences you use to fill your bucket you never feel fulfilled because of the holes, you are insatiable. If you are feeling a lack of that fulfillment you so desire, it may drive you to these unhealthy choices instead.

JOURNAL:

If you receive no Attention; instead ABSENCE, or your loved one is unavailable even when there, or they are preoccupied or they treat you as unimportant you may feel lonely, unworthy, unimportant. You may choose an AOC (Addictive Obsessive Compulsive) Response.
What might you choose?

_____

If you receive no Affection; instead ALOOFNESS, or your loved one is cold, distant, awkward, physically abusive or detached you may feel like you are a mistake or unlovable, ugly or undeserving. You may choose an AOC (Addictive Obsessive Compulsive) Response.
What might you choose?

_____

If you received no Acceptance; instead ABUSE, or your loved one is punitive, attacking, demanding, controlling or demeaning you may feel like you are stupid, bad, wrong, victimized, revengeful. You may choose an AOC (Addictive Obsessive Compulsive) Response.
What might you choose?

_____

If you received no Approval; instead ABANDONMENT, or your loved one claimed disappointment in you, or was distancing, disowning, dismissive or disgusted you may feel worthless, alone, separate. You may choose an AOC (Addictive Obsessive Compulsive) Response. What might you choose?

_____

If you received no Acknowledgement; instead ASSESSMENT, or your loved ones were judgmental, criticizing, made personal attacks or put downs you may feel incapable, ashamed and rebellious. You may choose an AOC (Addictive Obsessive Compulsive) Response. What might you choose?

_____

Now you understand the triggers that may cause you to attempt to fill the leaky buckets with things that do not serve you or your relationship, let's look at how we can take responsibility to repair these holes.

_____

REPAIRING THE HOLES / HEALING THE WOUNDS:

It is the feeling we have in reaction to these wounds that drive us to our addictive, obsessive or compulsive behaviors. These behaviors affect every area of our life.

JOURNAL

Let's look at the dreams we have for our lives that are sabotaged by these behaviors. Which AOC behavior do YOU use to sabotage these different areas of your life?

Career/Finance/Education:

_____

Relationships:

_____

Body/Mind/Spirit:

_____

Contribution:

_____

When we look outside of ourselves to fill the leaky bucket we can be on an endless quest to satiate the insatiable. The wounds that were inflicted to the inner child have festered in our "child mind" and have created a "dis-ease." Our natural tendencies are to use "stuff" to sooth the pain of the wound.

The solution is to heal these wounds which in turn repairs the leaky bucket and turns it into an open vessel. This allows us to be satisfied, grateful and aware of the fulfilling elements available in every loving experience or significant relationship. The effect of this is that we are no longer driven to look outside of ourselves to feed the unquenchable appetite of Addiction, Obsession & Compulsion.

Each of the 5 A's that were missing have their own distinct repair.

<u>The 5 A'S</u>   <u>The Repairs</u>

ATTENTION   AWARENESS (MENTAL)
AFFECTION   AMORE (PHYSICAL)
ACCEPTANCE   ACCOUNTABILIY (GROWTH)
APPROVAL   APPRECIATION(SPIRIT)
ACKNOWLEDGEMENT   AFFIRMATION (EMOTION)

When we are driven by our commitments, instead of our feelings we are more accomplished, satisfied and peaceful. In order to make the shift from being feelings driven to commitment driven we need to concentrate a small part of our day on repairing the holes in our buckets from childhood wounds.

REPAIRING THE HOLES IN THE BUCKET

AWARENESS (Mental healing)
Doing experiential personal growth work and reading books such as "The Journey to YOU" and "The Journey to US" along with will repair the hole caused by absence and the lack of attention.

AMORE (Physical healing)
Taking the best care of yourself with nutrition and massage and exercise will repair the hole caused by aloofness and the lack of affection.

ACCOUNTABILITY (Growth promotion)
Practicing taking 100% responsibility for every event in your life will repair the hole caused by abuse or the lack of acceptance.

APPRECIATION (Spiritual healing)
Being grateful for everything you have created for yourself will repair the hole caused by abandonment and lack of approval.

AFFIRMATION (Emotional healing)
Daily self-affirmations will repair the hole caused by assessment and the lack of acknowledgement.

JOURNAL

List the ways that you will repair the holes in your bucket:

Awareness _____
Amore _____
Accountability _____
Appreciation _____
Affirmation _____

Chapter 14.

WHAT IS IN YOUR WATER BOTTLE?

Please get a full 16 oz. water bottle. Put it in your non-dominant hand, stand up and hold your arm straight out parallel to the floor. On a scale of 1 to 10 how uncomfortable is it for your arm to hold the bottle? Keep it like that as you read this story, don't put it down.

There were two Buddhist Monks who were travelling a long distance to a Monastery. They had to cross a river, but when they approached the bridge, they saw that it had been washed away in a storm. There was a beautiful young woman in a lovely kimono who was crying by the remains of the bridge. One of the Monks asked her if she needed help and she said she needed to cross the river and didn't know how she would get across without ruining her lovely kimono since there was no bridge. The Monk picked her up, carried her across the river and placed her down on the opposite bank. The Monks continued on in silence toward their destination. Just when the Monastery was in sight, the other Monk turned to his companion and said "What you did was wrong, we are to stay away from women, and you carried her in your arms!" The kind Monk turned to him and replied "Are you still carrying that girl? I put her down hours ago."

Now, how uncomfortable is your arm on a scale of 1 – 10? What are you refusing to let go of? The longer you hold on to resentment the heavier it gets. Let it go. Every single day is a clean page, and you are the creator of what you fill your page with, closeness or distance.

BEST WAYS TO SABOTAGE YOUR RELATIONSHIP

1. INFIDELITY
2. BROKEN TRUST
3. THREAT OF DIVORCE
4. OBSTINANCE
5. EMOTIONAL NEGLECT
6. MONEY CONFLICTS
7. ADDICTIVE BEHAVIORS
8. SEPARATION
9. EMOTIONAL INFIDELITY
10. BOREDOM
11. POOR COMMUNICATION
12. NO SEX
13. LACK OF APPRECIATION
14. NO AFFECTION
15. NO ATTENTION
16. NO APPROVAL
17. NO ACCEPTANCE
18. NO ACKNOWLEDGEMENT
19. ABUSE

Let's take a look at each one of these 19 ways you can sabotage your relationship. Often, we are unaware at how detrimental some of our behavior is to our relationship. Awareness is step one.

INFIDELITY

Sexual infidelity is one of the most difficult violations to repair, but it is possible with both parties taking 100% responsibility, the willingness to communicate, listen and a new agreement between the partners. Boredom and not being each other's protagonist can be the cause. A large percentage of infidelity is caused through mutual experimentation as in the swinger mentality. That choice can damage or even destroy a marriage eventually. Remember couple A in the previous chapter who both took responsibility for the infidelity? That was the only way to repair the betrayal from infidelity.

BROKEN TRUST

Breaking your word consistently erodes trust, intimacy and respect. Breaking your word on marriage vows or important agreements has your partner be suspicious and untrusting and has them doubt whether they should be in the relationship at all. It leaves them looking for a plan "B." The way to solve this is to be clear about agreements; not all requests result in an agreement. If that is not clear, a request could look like a demand and create resentment without agreement. A request not satisfied can look like a broken agreement. The are some agreements in a partnership that if broken would be a deal breaker. You and your partner should discuss deal breakers, so you are both clear.

"Deal Breakers" are serious boundaries that if violated means the probable end of the marriage. The fewer 'deal breakers' you have as a couple, the better.

Some people think infidelity is a deal breaker. Something that may be a deal breaker for one person may not be a deal breaker for their partner. For some people taking drugs or alcohol after a long struggle with addiction and getting sober, may be a deal breaker.

Whatever your deal breakers are write them down in your Journal, then ask yourself "Would I end the relationship if my partner did that?" If the answer is yes, then that is a deal breaker. Physical violence is a deal breaker for anyone with self-respect. Make sure you always have a plan "B" so that no one can ever hold you hostage, in any area of your life. When you have a plan B you can always set boundaries from a place of strength.

THREAT OF DIVORCE
Use of this tactic is manipulative, controlling and abusive. Everything can be worked out with intention & communication. If your "Deal Breakers" are clear, then the threat of breaking up is unnecessary. Be careful; if you use this just to get your way, someday your partner may call your bluff. Using the phrase "maybe we just shouldn't be together is the red flag of my "way or the highway!"

The things people argue about most are money, sex and kids. Take a parenting course, like "Redirecting Children's Behavior," that does not advise the use of reward or punishment, get on the same page. Get financial counseling or take a course together on money management. Recreate your sex life being your essence. More on this later.

OBSTINANCE

When one partner is closed to requests, growth, listening to their partner's opinions, agreeing to disagree, etc., this erodes the desire of the other partner to even try. Communication becomes withholding instead, requests become demands or ultimatums; respect for each other's opinions becomes a condescending joke. To turn this around takes vulnerable communication and modeling the behavior you want from you're partner.

Those who have the attitude of 'my way or the highway' tend to be obstinate and controlling to the point of emotionally abusive. Those who refuse any self- correction, using the excuse that 'this is just the way I am,' are unyielding and closed. Those who say 'don't even talk to me about it,' who refuse to even listen or communicate, are being obstinate to the point of rather being right, in control and comfortable, all the egoic priorities, than being close or understood.

Most people have the mistaken belief that in order to make a relationship work it means you need to get the other person to agree with you. That will cause constant conflict. The goal for a healthy, loving functional relationship is to understand each other, not necessarily agree with each other. We need to work on being the best person we can be and allow our partner to be our protagonist in that effort. We will agree sometimes but what we need to strive for is to understand each other. "You be you and I'll be me, I will 'see' you and I will allow you to 'see' me.

EMOTIONAL NEGLECT

Disregarding your partner's needs, opinions, and requests or being disrespectful by your tone, attitude or way of being is emotional neglect. If we are treating our partner with any less regard or kindness than we treat our friends or co-workers, then we may be emotionally neglecting them. Most of why we argue is because of the tone of voice used, it is not what is said but it is how it is said. When your tone of voice is condescending, demeaning, critical or disgusted there is no room for closeness. The attitude and tone of the dismissive "whatever" response may have your partner feel stupid and unimportant. Ask yourself if that is what you intend.

MONEY CONFLICTS

When one person controls the money and is expected to budget, make sure everything is paid and handled on time the other partner is usually uninformed and left in the dark wondering why there isn't money for this and that. They may even sabotage the person taking care of the finances by spending irresponsibly or by making unreasonable requests and having expectations, resentment or becoming demanding. Herein lays the problem. A partnership occurs when both parties are involved in decision making, and both are informed; common goals are discussed regularly and issues, problems and spending habits are shared. It is the fear of scarcity that becomes the wedge between couples who have financial issues.

If you want to come together philosophically on the subject of money, there are a few things you can do. First take a money management course together, or go to a financial planner together to see what the best way to create abundance is. You could also watch the movie "The Secret" and pause it when you want to discuss what is being presented and just talk. You may come up with lots of new paradigms about money and the creation of abundance as a team. The next page is a list of philosophical beliefs of the people who experience true abundance. Discuss these concepts and distinctions of abundance with your partner.

Here are the 22 Distinctions of Abundance:

I. God is abundant in all things; I am a child of God, abundance, therefore, is my inheritance.

II. I use the vocabulary of abundance to attract all possibility of bounty.

III. As it is necessary for the tides of great oceans to ebb and flow so it is with great wealth. I trust that the wave always returns!

IV. I am surrounded with overflowing prosperity, visible and invisible. I open my arms to both give and receive.

V. I deserve to flourish in every area of my life. The desire to be affluent is only matched by my gratitude for everyone's abundance.

VI. I celebrate everyone else flourishing as I know that I am as worthy of opulence as they are.

VII. If I am breathing today, I have another chance to create a path to fertile ground no matter how many roads I have passed by before.

VIII. When others tell me "It can't be done" I say: "Well, I'm going to do it anyway, want to help?"

IX. I trust that every seed I plant will bloom exactly when I am ready for the bounty and no sooner.

X. I attract wealth in many different ways and in many forms. I do not need to know how to have it happen, I just need to be sure that I will figure it out.

XI. I contribute unconditionally knowing that the excitement of giving will attract even more resources, value and wealth for the giver and the receiver. I never lend, I instead give as much as I can give with no expectation, just gratitude that I am in a position to give.

XII. All abundance is attracted to loving thoughts, feelings and actions. All scarcity is attracted to fearful thoughts, feelings, and actions.

XIII. I inspire and empower others to pursue their own abundance, the karma bus drives in circles.

XIV. My prosperity will arrive in direct proportion as I believe it will. I give myself permission to believe I can have opulence.

XV. I remove all negative thoughts and beliefs about wealth, luxury and affluence. I realize that I will still be a person of integrity as a millionaire or a billionaire.

XVI. The most beloved and important people and experiences in my life will flourish around my abundance. I am grateful for and cherish each person and experience.

XVII. I am the happiest person I know. I choose the ways of being that would reflect that my goals and dreams have already happened as I continue on the path of creation. I surround myself with abundant and positive people.

XVIII. I am open to all resources. I share my vision with everyone I know and I am willing and grateful and excited to accept support.

XIX. I take 100% responsibility for all my results. I know that there is as much value in the gifts and lessons of setbacks as there is in success.

XX. I trust that my higher power and the universe are cooperating to guide me towards abundance every moment, even if the way it looks is a surprise!

XXI. I trust my inner voice as if it were my angel speaking to me. My intuition is at least as valuable as my knowledge.

XXII. I am willing to give and receive love and knowledge for the purpose of my own abundance and the success of those around me. Every transaction is a win-win.

Some of these philosophies may resonate with you; some may not. Just embrace what works for you and discard the rest and revisit them later.

Story #4 ~ Romance and Abundance!
Thank you, Rhonda and Steve!

A friend relayed this story to me. She and her husband are just an adorable and fun couple that everyone wants to be around. They flip homes, like the couples you see on TV and this was one of their date nights:

So... here's the thing... earlier today I was thinking I need to have a talk with Steve about the lack of romance in our relationship. I expected he would take me to some fancy restaurant, buy flowers, and do the cuddly movie thing. Well.... I didn't get a chance to tell him that but he said: "Let's go eat." We were going to go to a restaurant but it was crowded and the line was a mile long.

So instead we went to Waffle House. Our server was a sweet lady. She seemed to have some small type of disability but was fast; she made sure our food was perfect, and didn't miss a beat.

If my eyes were shut, the service standards could have been confused with any fine dining. Of course, the food was good. I haven't had Waffle House in years, love breakfast. So, we pay with $100 bill and she seemed upset because she couldn't make change for our $17 tab. My husband told her to keep the change. She blinked and assumed we were teasing. She offered to walk across to the gas station for change. He said, "No, seriously, that's for you." She asked three times if he was serious. She could not believe it. Most romantic date ever!!! I love him so much. Back to our roots of why I fell in love with him in the first place.

ADDICTIVE BEHAVIORS

When addiction is an issue in a relationship the first rule is "Work on Your own" by repairing those holes and seeking whatever support you may need. We are a society of addicts; everyone has some issue: sex, drugs, alcohol, shopping, gambling, credit cards, food, pornography, the internet, etc. By scrutinizing our partner, we avoid looking at our own need for growth, healing and recovery. Setting clear boundaries about someone else's addictive behavior that affects you or the relationship is your right and should be done without anger, shame or blame.

Be kind but firm when setting boundaries about addiction. Being vague about the consequences of someone's addictive behavior just gives them a back door.

We all have some addictive behaviors. Being each other's protagonists means asking our partner what we can do to support them. It may mean getting help together, or it may mean allowing your partner to explore what works for them without condemnation. It all depends on the level of disruption that the addictive behavior brings to the relationship. Remember, every couple is different, you need to find out what works for you. Try working on repairing the holes in your bucket and supporting your partner to do the same.

SEPARATION

Avoiding each other in any way is creating separation. List the ways you avoid closeness & intimacy and just agree to transform half that time into creating intimacy. Read to each other instead of reading alone, watch TV that you both enjoy and record the shows you don't like to watch together to watch when your partner is busy, cook together, share chores that used to "belong" to one person. Take walks together instead of separate gyms, spot each other at the gym, for every trip you must take apart plan one together, even for a day. Look for activities that you can enjoy together and plan as many as you can. This is a way to fill that relationship account.

EMOTIONAL INFIDELITY

This is the most common form of cheating. Even if you would never think of sexual infidelity you may be emotionally unfaithful and not even be aware.

Example: Talking about your partner in a disparaging way to someone in your confidence, replacing your partner with a friend or co-worker to share intimate thoughts or secrets, sharing about your partner to someone else vs. sharing with them. This can lead to sexual infidelity too.

When partners neglect each other emotionally, or they do not live with an intention to stay connected, or to be interesting, exciting or romantic, then often one, or both partners looks for excitement elsewhere. I have seen couples that really did love each other, they really did value their relationship, they never did cheat, physically, but they became very connected with someone else because they were looking for something that was missing, something that they longed for.

Life is short, when people start feeling like they are being denied something they may reach out in an attempt to fill that bucket, in a way that they would never guess they would. Sometimes people find themselves in the middle of a very passionate emotional affair that threatens their relationship with their partner. They either don't want it to end, they don't know how to end it, or they want it to go further. It is much easier to avoid the conditions that would cause an emotional affair than it is to solve the issue after it has developed.

Open, healthy communication where there is as much listening as there is revealing, about your partner's needs, desires, dreams and hopes could be the beginning of creating what is needed to keep both partners satisfied. One person said if my partner had just been willing to really listen to me, or if my partner had been open to more sex, it would have helped me not need to look for closeness elsewhere.

BOREDOM

Boredom is the cause of couples breaking up who have been together for years, seemingly happy and who never argue. Then one day one of you come home and says "I'm leaving, I found someone else, I love you but I'm not in love with you." "Who is it?" you ask. "It's my co-worker." "What?" You exclaim, "That person you always fight with?" "Yes, I am challenged by them, it's exciting!" Ending boredom takes more that going out on dates, no matter where you go you take you with you.

Give your partner the 5 "A"s, listen (with popcorn) when they talk, use the best tools you have to communicate, challenge each other, be each others protagonist, share problems, insights, knowledge & opinions with each other, keep your sex life fun. People who are bored in their relationships are boring themselves, looking for a partner to create excitement instead of taking responsibility to be the creator.

POOR COMMUNICATION

This will erode a relationship like a slow death.
Examples of poor communication are:

1. Interrupting. When you interrupt someone who is speaking, it is sending the message that "what I have to say is more important than what you are saying."

   That disrespect creates an energy between you that is not conducive to valuing each other or listening. Also, when you interrupt someone they cannot hear what you are saying because their brain is occupied holding on to the thought that was interrupted.

2. Badgering. This is verbal and emotional abuse to continue to badger someone until they give up their point of view and agree with you. Remember the goal of communication is NOT to get your partner to agree with you but it is about getting your partner to understand you and for you to understand them.

3. Righteousness. The need to be right can destroy any relationship. Righteousness has an attitude and a tone of voice that basically communicates that your partner is wrong. Strive for understanding and acceptance instead of being right.

4. Condescension. When you disagree with your partner and then take on an air of superiority, distain, disrespect or patronizing in order to make your partner feel stupid for disagreeing with you, that shuts down communication and creates resentment.

5. Name Calling. Personal attacks and name calling will create an adversarial atmosphere, that makes the relationship look like a war instead of love.

6. Demanding. When one person demands agreement by threatening or manipulating the relationship is fear-driven, not motivated by love.

7. Controlling. When one partner needs to always be in control they will use very manipulative tactics including the silent treatment to get their way. This erodes relationships and makes the people in relationship with a controlling partner long for their own personal freedom.

8. Discounting. When one partner's needs are minimized and discounted, if they are in conflict with the other partner's needs, then one person's self-esteem is damaged as they feel small and unimportant and may fall into a depression.

9. Fixing. When one partner often needs to fix what they consider the imperfections of the other partner that makes them feel like they are incapable and they are a mistake themselves. "Supporting" a partner means to assist when asked. "Helping" is for the purpose of making your partner feel helpless so that the "fixer" can feel superior.

10. Criticizing. Constant criticism, including personal attacks, destroys someone's spirit. People who are criticized end up feeling worthless, and unlovable.

11. Bringing up history. Using the constant referring back to past mistakes as a manipulation tactic prevents anyone in the relationship from learning from mistakes, growing and taking responsibility. Instead, sharing with each other, the gifts and lessons from the process supports both parties to learn.

12. Jealousy. In some extreme cases, jealousy is a type of mental illness like paranoid delusions. It can also be a sign of a physical disease that causes delusions. The other possibility is that the person who is jealous is actually the person who is considering cheating and their guilt about that makes them want to justify their desires by accusing their partner of the same breach of trust.

Jealousy can also be caused by some historical filter that was formed when you or your partner had an experience of infidelity or a failed relationship due to an affair. The other possibility which is the least likely is: Your partner is cheating.

I knew a couple who were both big flirts and both very secure in their marriage. Cheating was a deal breaker, but they had agreed at the beginning of their relationship that if they were attracted to someone else that they would tell their partner, or they would bring any sexual energy they had on someone back to their own bedroom and "take it out on each other."

That may not work for everyone, but it worked great for them, and they did not have an issue with jealousy. Remember, you are the creator!

If there is some extreme and unfounded jealousy it is advisable to consult a therapist or an MD as one of the symptoms of Parkinson's and some other diseases is delusional jealousy.

13. Anger. People who have anger issues see themselves as victims. If we all practice taking 100% responsibility for everything in our lives we are no longer angry. Searching for the gifts and lessons attached to each experience makes us wiser, more mature, more powerful, and less angry!

14. Blame. Looking for whose fault something may be, is just another way to be a victim. Even if we blame ourselves and say "that was my FAULT" we are victimizing ourselves! Taking responsibility instead means we look and see what we could have done differently, what would we do differently next time something like this happens and looking at what we were supposed to learn so that we do not need to continue to repeat history. The more responsibility we take in our lives and our relationships the more control we have, the more power we have and the more freedom we have.

15. Judgment. When instead of giving our partner acceptance of who they are and the journey they are on we judge them, we make it unsafe for them to share anything with us.

    A couple came to me complaining that they could not talk to each other. I asked them why not. They said they always got into a fight when they tried to talk. Here is what was happening. They were judging each other and it showed up in their tone of voice.

    When they began to practice just listening for the purpose of understanding each other it made acceptance much easier.

Remember, it is not our job to convince our partner to agree with us, it is our job to understand them and make sure they understand us. No one wants to be judged.

16. Shut down. "It's like talking to a wall." When we shut down it leaves our partner feeling unimportant, disconnected and alone. When we feel alone for long enough we keep asking ourselves, why not just be alone instead of putting up with the rejection since we already feel alone. If you need time to think or process just tell your partner that and make an agreement as to when in the near future you would be willing to communicate.

17. Grudge holding. The "silent treatment" is meant to punish your partner when you did not get your way about something. This punishes the grudge holder as much as their partner.

    A couple once told the story to me about when one of them loved holding grudges. The problem was that the other partner wasn't controlled or manipulated by that at all, they were just not a very good co-dependent. So, one day when the grudge holder was in full revenge mode the rest of the family was planning on going to the movies. The grudge holder's partner said, "I understand you are angry and if you need to hold on to that it's fine but you will need to stay home.

The children and I are going to the movies and if you can shift your attitude I would love for you to come with us but if you need to stay angry, I understand. We are leaving in fifteen minutes."

The grudge holder at that point decided that staying resentful did not serve anyone, there was a shift in attitude and they all enjoyed the day together. Later the couple did discuss the breakdown and came to a better understanding of each other.

18. Ignoring. When people are spending time with their spouse, but they still feel alone it is because they are being ignored. We all need to feel heard.

Spending just 10 minutes a day listening to each other solves this problem. Just ask questions and listen for 10 minutes a day and you will be amazed at the miraculous improvement in your communication and the relationship.

JOURNAL:

Write a list of ways that you both sabotage communication with your partner.

Ways to open up communication are:

1. Being a generous listener, ask questions that make it safe for your partner to expand their ability to reveal.

2. Be attentive, don't do anything but listen when your partner is talking, give eye contact.

3. If it is a difficult or emotional subject hold hands while talking.

4. Look for win-wins if you are problem solving together.

5. Acknowledge each other, express approval, use the time you have to communicate as an opportunity to let your partner know what you appreciate about them and why you are grateful for them.

6. Be kind to each other when a mistake has been made. "Everyone makes mistakes" is a wonderful comment that promotes acceptance, one of the most important and most challenging things to give in a relationship.

7. Be respectful of each other's right to set boundaries.

8. Agree to disagree, remember, the goal is to understand each other, not to always agree.

9. Validate by repeating what you heard. "What I heard you say is …." This will have your partner feel heard and is a way to eliminate yelling. Often people get louder if they feel as if they have not been heard!

10. Create ground rules for fighting. Everyone argues, as long as you have ground rules to prevent abuse and disrespect your arguments can actually bring you closer instead of more distant. You need to design what rules for fighting work for YOU but here are some ground rules that other couples have adopted:

    A. Move to a private space to argue, not in public or in front of children.
    B. Wait until we are not angry.
    C. Come to an understanding before bed.
    D. Stay on the subject, no history.
    E. No personal attacks.
    F. Ask for what you want
    G. Take some time to calm down and then come back and finish.

JOURNAL:

Write down what you want your rules for fighting to be. Ask your partner to write down the rules they would like for fighting. Compare them when complete and talk about adopting the ones you have in common, or the ones you both agree with, as your own.

NO SEX

This can be a huge red flag. Unless you have decided to adapt celibacy as a part of a spiritual path, this is unnatural. Couples who do not have sex may be suffering from either a physical or psychological problem that needs to be addressed through communication and sometimes outside support.

See a doctor if the problem is physical or a therapist if it is emotional. A sign of depression is lack of interest in sex. People who have been violated sexually, either as a child who has been molested, an adult who has been raped or in a dysfunctional relationship, may have issues creating the emotional intimacy needed to connect in a sexual way.

Physical symptoms that prevent enjoyable sex are an indication that something else may be going on with your health that may need a doctor's care. If the reason a couple does not have sex is because there are problems in the relationship this book should help if you actually use some of the tools provided. Read it to each other at night. There are people who just have no interest in sex and have come to an unspoken agreement that sex is not necessary in their relationship. If this is the case there really should be some discussion about it so that you both know it is a conscious decision, not just an avoidance of intimacy.

To prevent boredom in your sexual relationship there are many books that can give you fun ways to enjoy yourself. One is called "101 Nights of Great Sex" by Laura Corn. A book that may increase the intimacy that leads to sex is "101 Nights of Great Romance" by the same author. Remember, for most women; Intimacy leads to sex. For most men; Sex leads to intimacy. But often those gender norms are reversed. Whining or being grumpy because you have not had sex lately is not a form of foreplay, foreplay needs to start 24 hours before the act with caressing, kissing, massage, kind words, delivering the 5 "A"s.

If you have not had sex for a long time just because you are busy and tired and distracted, the usual reasons why people stop being physical here are four things you can do to start that engine up again.

1. Deliver the 5 "A"s everyday: Attention, Affection, Acceptance, Approval and Acknowledgement.

2. Talk about sex when you are not in a position to actually have sex like in a restaurant, over the phone, in the car. Talking about what kind of sex you enjoy giving and receiving in a positive, flirty way, opens up the hormonal pathways.

3. Give yourselves permission to talk about fantasies, even ones that you would not do in real life but talking about them can be a turn on.

4. Pick one day a week that you are willing to have sex, even if you need to start slowly by just talking about what you'd like to do, that's fine, but keep that date.

5. Make sure that you are working on open, loving, accepting communication with your partner. Feeling heard and understood is the best aphrodisiac.

LACK OF APPRECIATION

Work on "mastery" in your relationship by reducing expectations to increase the gratitude you have and express. Expectation gives birth to disappointment. Having expectations of your partner is manufacturing premeditated resentment.

What makes it worse is that most expectations are unspoken! Unless you met your partner at a psychic fair you need to ask for what you want and create agreement! Without expectation there is only gratitude.

Expectation sounds like "What's for dinner?" Appreciation sounds like "Mmmm something smells wonderful. Are you making dinner? Thank you so much!"

Practice being grateful by verbally acknowledging even the smallest acts of love like: cooking, food shopping, a look, a touch, going out to work, caring for children.

Having no expectations is the holy grail of relationships, strive to recognize whenever you have expectations and work on releasing them in favor of appreciation. This does not mean you can use this as an excuse to break your agreements in the name of "My partner should not have expected me to keep it!" That is manipulation.

NO AFFECTION
Your relationship should be your number one priority. Kids grow up and leave, if you have not made the relationship your priority you will look at each other when becoming empty nesters and say "Who are you?" If you lose your job, business or home, you will still have your partner if you have made your relationship a priority.

A clear sign indicating if you are doing this is your level of affection. Do you seem to be in love to your friends, kids, family? Do you touch when passing each other, do you take a few seconds to hug, kiss, or rub each other's shoulders, head, hands, feet? You know what your partner likes as a show of affection, look for opportunities to touch, hold hands etc.

This can also create intimacy but pure affection should not be a tactic to get sex although it does create an opening for the possibility! It takes less than 10 seconds to deliver some affection. Start by giving your partner a 10 second hug every day. See how powerful it is to melt into each other's arms and feel that love and safety that brought you together in the first place.

NO ATTENTION

Make specific dates to be together, make your relationship a priority. It is imperative that you spend focused time together with the intention of giving each other the attention that you both deserve. Make dates to spend time together, even if it is just at home.

To make sure that you are delivering the attention that is imperative to having a healthy relationship here are four suggestions:

1. Spend 10 minutes a day asking your partner about their day, their experiences, their feelings, their friends or whatever they are involved with and just listen!

2. Make a weekly date night that is spent together doing whatever you both enjoy, board games, watch movies, read to each other, dance in the living room. Take turns who plans the date each week.
3. Make plans together for a monthly 'day trip' together that you both would enjoy. EG: a picnic in the park, a hike in the woods, drive to the water, movie marathon.
4. Plan a yearly vacation together. Even if money is an issue, challenge yourself to do a low cost or free vacation.

EG: Tent camping, visit friends or relatives in another town who have a guest room, volunteer with a mission trip. Being together doing something different and interesting that will create bonds, closeness and connection. That is the important part. Of course, if you can afford a week at the amazing Grove Park Inn in Asheville, go for it! Make sure to be there for their world-famous Sunday brunch!

NO ACCEPTANCE

Agree to disagree, accept each other's humanity and each other's unique Journey. The opposite of acceptance is judgement. If you are not being accepting of your partners quirks, issues, opinions or mistakes then you are sending the message that you are judging them as bad, wrong, stupid, whatever.

That makes it very unsafe to talk to you and be honest and revealing. Judgement created distance. Just because you are accepting and because you strive to understand your partner does not mean you are approving of everything they are doing. But it does mean that your partner will be better able to trust you to share their challenges and thoughts with you. Acceptance creates safety to communicate which creates closeness.

NO APPROVAL

Notice your partner's efforts and accomplishments. When we know that we are appreciated and our results get noticed we are happier and more motivated. One way to have someone fall in love with you is to ask them what their goals and dreams are and notice when they take action to accomplish them or when they finally achieve them. This is as simple as saying good job, or thank you for that effort, or wow, outstanding work!

NO ACKNOWLEDGEMENT

Verbalize everything you appreciate about your partner, their strengths, talents and character. In the movie Avatar, the two main characters did not say "I love you" to each other, they said, "I see you." Your partner wants to know you value them and why.

If you have neglected acknowledging your partner for a long time when you start doing this they may be less than receptive.

If they seem closed when you acknowledge them it may be because they have wanted you to "See" them for so long that they gave up wanting it, and became resentful that it seems as though they are not appreciated. Start slowly, with just one acknowledgement per day. Then you can increase that once they become comfortable with receiving the acknowledgement.

ABUSE: There are many ways to abuse each other. Physical abuse should not be tolerated under any circumstances by either party! A joking slap, punch on the arm, etc. is abuse. Set boundaries immediately make it a deal breaker! Here are some other forms of abuse:

1. The very first and most common sign of abuse is isolating someone by cutting them off from friends and family. This makes the partner of the abuser dependent on them for everything, companionship, help, money, everything. That makes it easier for the abuser to control and manipulate them.

2. Abusers interrogate their partners in a way that is hostile, repetitive and controlling.

3. Abusers have lots of expectations, and they get livid if they are not met. They also have a sense of ownership of their partner: You are MY spouse now, you have to abide by what I want.

That is why often abusers will sweep the partner off their feet and rush to marry them because they think then they will have complete dominance over their partner.

4. Badgering until their partner relents is another sign. This looks like nagging, demanding and threatening.

5. Abusers force their opinion on their partner by getting angry if they do not get an agreement.

6. Abusers use money to control and create dependency so the partner feels helpless to stand up for themselves.

7. Abusers criticize, humiliate and attack their partners appearance. They say things like "Well, if you weren't so fat" or "Why don't you get a boob job." This is meant to make their partner feel like they are not enough to ever be in any other relationship so they might as well tolerate the abuser.

8. Abusers undermine self-confidence and self-esteem. They say put downs like "You would be nothing without me" or "You would never be able to get through nursing school." This makes the partner feel incapable of ever standing on their own two feet and makes them think they need the abuser.

9. The abuser will in fits of rage get physically violent with property and destroy their partner possessions. This message is "You better do what I want or your head will be the next thing I break" so they can keep the partner in fear.

10. Abusers use a communication tactic that keeps the partner on egg shells. They use personal attacks to put the partner down, they will use name calling, they will blame use sarcasm which is a cutting remark intended to wound. Abusers like an audience to humiliate the partner too and make them the butt of contempt or ridicule. The worst part is that they are very good at making this all look like playing, a joke, just their sense of humor so they can get away with it.

11. Abusers use threats to create fear and danger. It sometimes sounds like "I will take those kids and you will never see them again."

12. Abusers disregard their partners needs or opinions. They treat them as unimportant and unintelligent.

13. Abusers often make unwanted or inappropriate sexual advances. They treat their partner like they own them and if they want sex then they should just be able to demand it. They will get very angry if they are often refused sex and may intimate that they can get it elsewhere as a threat. This is like rape by intimidation.

If you recognize this treatment in your own relationship, don't think this will get better or go away by ignoring it. It won't. Abuse normally gets worse until it is totally unmanageable. There are a few things you need to do.

First, you need a plan B. Everyone should have a plan B for every area of your life, your career, your relationships and your living situation. If you have a plan B no one can hold you hostage. A plan B is valuable not just in case of needing to escape abuse but sometimes there are very unexpected circumstance that arise and having a plan B gives people dealing with difficulties peace and confidence.

Second, you need to find support for yourself. A therapist, a personal growth course, books, like this one, investigating relationship tools, or a life coach for yourself or at least a good friend to talk to.

I don't always advise going to a marriage counselor with the abuser. That can actually make things worse. When a marriage counselor starts asking tough questions it can infuriate and humiliate the abuser, and they will take out their anger on the partner that brought them there.

Often a marriage counselor wants to look at the past and what has happened to "settle" the disagreements. A good life coach, or counselor, will ask you where you are right now and where you want to be.

They will give you tools and coaching to get from where you are to where you want to be. It is a different philosophy. The point is, get support for yourself, if the abuser wants support they will find it, but usually, they do not.

If you don't think you are worthy of saving yourself just remember, your children are watching. They will recreate your relationship because they will choose a partner just like you or the one you chose. Who do you want them to be? Be that person yourself. What kind of a partner do you want them to have? Be that kind of partner yourself. Those little eyes are always watching and deciding that what they are witnessing is what love should look like.

Remember abuse is gender neutral.

Chapter 15

Sometimes we have different priorities than just being close. Let's look at what other priorities there can be in a relationship, what they look like and what can be done to transform them to having the priorities of understanding, support and intimacy instead.

The mistaken priorities in marriage are:
- being a martyr
- being superior
- being in control
- looking good
- being comfortable
- punishing

When someone has a priority of being a MARTYR they are feeling used or victimized. What they need to do to redirect their own behavior is to ask for what they want without using guilt to manipulate their partner. When your partner is in the mode of being a martyr you feel wrong or bad. If you want to redirect your partner's behavior when they are in the mode of martyr you can say "I feel like I am being blamed, tell me what you want." People who are often in the mode of martyr have a difficult time asking for what they want, and they have worthiness issues. They need lots of acknowledgement to feel deserving of asking for what they want.

When someone has a priority of BEING SUPERIOR they are feeling better than their partner but at the same time lonely. What they need to do to redirect their own behavior is to be vulnerable and revealing with their partner. When your partner is in the mode of superiority you feel unneeded, worthless and in some way less than your superior partner. If you want to redirect your partner's behavior when they are in the mode of superiority you can say "Let me know how I can support you, we are partners." People who are often in the mode of superiority have a difficult time asking for support because they don't believe they will actually get the support they want. They need lots of approval to feel like their partner is on their team.

When someone has a priority of BEING IN CONTROL they are feeling panicked and out of control. What they need to do to redirect their own behavior is to learn to delegate, trust and receive. When your partner is in the mode of being in control, you feel managed or challenged. If you want to redirect your partner's behavior when they are in the mode of being in control you can say "let's get calm and talk about this." People who are often in the mode of control have difficulty trusting that anyone can be as capable as they are. They need lots of acceptance they need to be given permission to be in charge often.

When someone has a priority of LOOKING GOOD or being impressive they are feeling a need to be liked and often confused as to how to please everyone. What they need to do to redirect their own behavior is to get very clear on what it is that they want and the boundaries they need to set. When your partner is in the mode of looking good or people-pleasing you feel burdened with too much control, including making your partner feel good about themselves. If you want to redirect your partner's behavior when they are in the mode of looking good, you can say "Tell me what you really want." People who are often in the mode of looking good are afraid of being judged, making mistakes or being wrong. They don't like taking responsibility or making decisions. They need permission to make mistakes, encouragement to make decisions and acceptance when they do, whatever the result may be.

When someone has a priority of COMFORT, they are feeling unmotivated or entitled. What they need to do to redirect their own behavior is to stretch, contribute daily and be vision driven. When your partner is in the mode of being comfortable, you feel angry, alone, burdened with all the responsibilities and frustrated. If you want to redirect your partner's behavior when they are in the mode of comfort you can stop care-taking and set boundaries being clear about what you are willing to take care of and what you are not willing to.

People who are often in the mode of comfort have a difficult time getting motivated, and they come from an entitled background where too much was done for them. They need lots of encouragement that their effort is needed and appreciated, and they need approval when they do contribute.

When someone has a priority of being a PUNISHER, they are feeling hurt and revengeful. What they need to do to redirect their own behavior is to take responsibility for whatever it is they are hurt about, and they need to communicate whatever they are upset about, and they need to set clear boundaries. When your partner is in the mode of being a punisher, you feel hurt, and in revenge too. Revenge is a cycle. If you want to redirect your partner's behavior when they are in the mode of punisher, you can encourage them to vent and listen for the purpose of understanding them. You will also need to repair any mistakes that may have hurt your partner. People who are often in the mode of punisher see themselves as a victim and someone who is abused and who wants to lash out and abuse their partner back. They need lots of open, safe, expressive conversation and to be understood.

Chapter 16.

It is really important to surround yourself with everything that brings you peace and comfort. As a couple you need to decide what brings you joy and encourage each other to surround yourselves with those things.

My husband and I both love art. We have so many pieces of art that were done by relatives or that we acquired at art shows ourselves that we have to rotate them because we don't have enough walls. We both love music but very different genres although we appreciate each other's tastes. We both like antiques and each surround ourselves with a few special collections. We really enjoy traveling and movies, too. I love photography and he is a wonderful photographer. We consciously surround ourselves with beauty and with everything that makes life more enjoyable and when you do that it makes the little stuff not matter. People tend to do less arguing and nit picking when they surround themselves with beauty.

Having a common vision or just knowing each other's vision so that you can make sure to support that visions infuses your relationship with freedom, encouragement, dreams and appreciation of your true partnership with a protagonist that cares about you realizing your dreams.

JOURNAL:

Journal the vision you have for your life with your partner:

1. in the very near future
2. Within a year
3. Within ten years
4. In your retirement years

Share what you wrote with your partner. Ask for suggestions, see if they resonate with the vision you have for your future.

Make plans to do a vision board together.
A vision board creates clarity so that you both know how to be better protagonists for each other. Sharing a vision is very intimate conversation, it usually happens as "pillow talk" or vacation dreaming. Making a vision board cements that vision into an everyday reminder.

Sharing your personal vision with your partner is just as important as sharing your goals as a couple and a family.

Sharing a vision keeps you connected and gives you a sense that you are not alone, you have a real partner in life. It also can keep you excited about life in general. It is always important that we all have something to look forward to. Knowing each other's personal vision too can keep you accountable and encourage you to take action because your partner can be your cheerleader too.

I always delight in hearing my children and their spouses brag about each other's accomplishments; I can tell they had been cheerleaders for each other which just adds so much joy to the accomplishments.

HOW TO MAKE YOUR VISION BOARD

1. Set an appointment with your partner
2. Start by talking about how you want to do it
3. Talk about what experience you are looking for
4. Talk about what feelings you are wanting to create
5. Be brave, get specific about what you want
6. Rip out photos from magazines or print some out
7. Encourage each other, don't be a control freak
8. Divide it into four areas
   A. Career/Finances/Education
   B. Your Relationships, with others too.
   C. Yourself, Body/Mind/Spirit
   D. Being a Contribution in the world

Get creative and know that every time you think about your vision, write down your vision, speak about your vision or make a vision board you are manifesting that vision!

Reading books together is a great way to keep growing and keep the lines of communication open. If you don't like reading use the time you have in a car together on trips to play audio books. Pause them when you want to talk about something from the book then continue listening. Here are some books that are valuable for couples:

The Journey to YOU by Tina Crumpacker
The Four Agreement by Don Miguel Ruiz
The Five Love Languages by Gary Chapman
The Secret by Rhonda Byrne
Co-dependent No More by Melody Beattie
101 Great Nights of Romance by Laura Corn
101 Great Nights of Sex by Laura Corn
Emotional Intelligence by Daniel Goleman
Any books by Harville Hendrix
Redirecting Children's Behavior by Katheryn Kvols

THINGS WE CAN LEARN FROM A DOG

Author Unknown

- Never pass up the opportunity to go for a joy ride together. Allow the experience of fresh air and the wind in your face to be pure ecstasy.
- When loved ones come home, always run to greet them.
- When you want treats practice obedience.
- Let others know when they've invaded your territory.
- Take naps together and stretch before rising.
- Run, romp and play daily.
- Be loyal.
- If what you want lies buried, dig until you find it.
- When someone is having a bad day, be silent, sit close by and nuzzle them gently.
- Thrive on the attention and let people touch you.
- Avoid biting when a simple growl will do.
- When you're happy, dance around and wag your entire body.
- No matter how often you're scolded, don't buy into the guilt thing and pout... Run right back and make friends
- Delight in the simple joy of a long walk together.
- Love each other unconditionally.

The Journey to US has been about Unique Solutions to create the fingerprint that is your relationship.

Here are 56 Unique Solutions.

1. Set your clear intention for your relationship.
2. Use these Unique Solutions to create a rare union.
3. Ask daily: Am I creating closeness or distance?
4. Speak about what you DO want NOT about what you don't want.
5. Choose to come from LOVE instead of fear.
6. Get uncomfortable to create something new.
7. Know and support each other's vision.
8. Read your intention for the relationship, daily.
9. Be each other's protagonist.
10. Thank your partner for being your protagonist.
11. Shift your attitude if yours is not working.
12. Become self-aware to identify when you are acting out of your ego or your essence.
13. Be the captain of your own ship by deciding what way of being you will choose with others.
14. Work on your own growth, not your partner's.
15. Choose to experience sex as your pure essence.
16. Practice transitioning from ego to essence.
17. Write a love letter for any special occasion instead of a card.
18. Strive for excellence, not perfection.

19. Give up your expectations, verbalize gratitude.
20. Ask for what you want and create agreements.
21. Give up ownership and control of your partner.
22. Fill up your relationship tank with kind deeds.
23. Be revealing and vulnerable to create closeness.
24. Plan and agreed time for difficult conversations.
25. Touch each other and use eye contact when communicating.
26. Work on your own vision and balance.
27. Accept each other's feelings to make communication safe.
28. Accept each other's opinions for the purpose of understanding instead of forcing agreement.
29. Respect the rules for fighting you agreed to.
30. Warn your partner when you need to vent.
31. Just listen, with popcorn, when your partner needs to vent.
32. Agree to come back and finish the argument if you need to take a break to get calm.
33. Set clear boundaries when you are calm.
34. Accept each other's quirks.
35. Ask "What did you hear me say" to create clear communication.
36. Accept advice from your protagonist.
37. Use a tone of voice that creates closeness instead of distance.

38. Take 100% Responsibility, look for the lessons so you don't need to repeat them.
39. Instead of apologies share how you created the breakdown the lessons you learned and what will be different.
40. Stop blaming and looking for whose fault something is, just own it.
41. Give up the need to be right for the goal of being understood and to understand.
42. Give up the need to be comfortable in order to create something new in your life.
43. Give up the need to be in control to create freedom and trust in your relationship.
44. Give up the need to impress others or be perfect to intentionally live as your pure essence.
45. No matter what feelings or emotions you are feeling choose loving actions.
46. Live in the present and stop punishing your partner for how others hurt you.
47. Share your feelings for the purpose of closeness but take action based on your commitment.
48. Give your partner these 5 "A"s every day: Attention, Affection, Acceptance, Approval and Acknowledgement
49. Repair the wounds of your past by giving yourself these 5 "A"s: Awareness, Amore, Accountability, Appreciation, Affirmation
50. Be aware of how you are sabotaging your relationship and choose closeness instead.

51. Use the tools to open up communication and to continue to create deeper intimacy.
52. Know the signs of abuse, don't tolerate it and have a plan "B" to stay safe.
53. Know how to redirect your own mistaken priorities and how to redirect your partner too.
54. Surround yourself with everything beautiful that brings you peace and joy to stay positive.
55. Keep working on your vision as a team.
56. Keep growing and learning together.

Just a reminder ~ Love Promises:

I promise to remind myself daily of my intentions and that this relationship is sacred. I promise to be grateful for what is working as well as for the lessons you, my protagonist, teach me. I promise to take responsibility and to redirect myself when possible. I also promise to be as open, honest and authentic as my humanity will allow, and to choose love over fear. I promise to strive for balance, ask permission, accept your feelings, keep the rules we agree to, vent when I need to, just listen when you need to vent, set clear boundaries, accept your quirks, encourage you, ask for what I want, and accept your advice. I promise to be led by my commitment, to work on my own growth and show you my love for you. I promise to be fun and considerate and to dance.

Recap of the importance of the 5 "A"s

The five things needed for a healthy loving functional relationship with anyone are:
#1: Affection (touch, not just sex), loving touch of any kind, even in business people touch, shake hands when they meet, touch a shoulder of a colleague.
#2: Attention: Quality time together, listening, making that person feel as if they are the only person on the planet in the moments you are with them, eye contact, don't allow interruptions during time together.
#3. Acceptance: Accept the other person's opinions, quirks, challenges, issues and most of all accept mistakes, everyone makes them. Acceptance is the key to open safe communication.
#4. Approval: Just noticing any action, effort or result the other person is creating. Mention it and praise them for a good job, good effort, good idea.
#5. Acknowledgement: Notice who they ARE, their character, their talent.

Remember the movie "Avatar?" The big blue people said "I see you." not I love you. Notice the character traits they have and let them know you see them AND you love them. The talents they possess are important too, "You are such a generous and creative partner, I am so grateful for you, I LOVE how artistic you are, you make everything look beautiful, and I want you to know I see it, I appreciate and love you."